MINISTRY IN TEARS

International Priests' Missionary Life and Ministry

REV. DASAN V VIMA; REV. BENJAMIN A VIMA

Order this book online at www.trafford.com
or email orders@trafford.com

Most Trafford titles are also available at major online book retailers.

Scripture quotations marked NASB are taken from the New American
Standard Bible, copyright 1960, 1962, 1963, 1968, 1971, 1972, 1973, 1975,
1977, and 1995 by the Lockman Foundation. Used with permission.

Print information available on the last page.

ISBN: 978-1-4907-6669-0 (sc)
ISBN: 978-1-4907-6670-6 (e)

Library of Congress Control Number: 2015919929

Trafford rev. 12/02/2015

 www.trafford.com
North America & international
toll-free: 1 888 232 4444 (USA & Canada)
fax: 812 355 4082

Contents

DEDICATION

With deepest sense of appreciation and gratitude, we dedicate this book to all our superiors and mentors, without whom we won't be what we are now. Though we would have misunderstood them sometimes as sharp "blades," we avow today they were the "ladders" through which we have reached this high level of integrity, honesty, dedication, and well-disciplined and properly balanced mind-set in our missionary services for the greater glory of God and for the fuller life of humanity.

The Priestly Tears

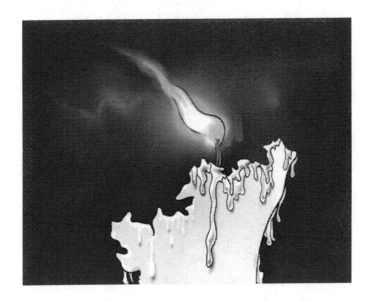

Fr. Benjamin Vima (Ben):

Tears are nothing but drops of saline continuously secreted between the surface of the eyes and the eyelids. A tear is basically water and salt, along with a little calcium and a few other chemicals that help lubricate our eyes. These watery drops are provided by nature to moisten and lubricate the outward parts of the eyes and keep them clear of foreign particles. What is a tear anyway? Mostly they are generated in response to any irritation of the eyes. In addition to this bodily fact, strong internal emotions of humans—such as joy, sorrow, elation, awe, and even fear and pleasure—produce such tears. These tears that flow from and inside our eyes, are, though mostly physical and emotional, sometimes generated by the human soul (spirit).

In general, this production of tears is increased due to strong emotional stress, pleasure, anger, suffering, mourning, or physical pain. However, it is not exclusively due to negative emotions; many people cry when extremely happy, such as during times of intense humor and laughter and at the exultant outbursts of feelings of gratitude (Ref. Skorucak A., "The Science of Tears," ScienceIQ.com).

Some years back, I read in an Indian newspaper that even animals do cry of triumph and suffering. I watched on TV a herd of elephants exhibiting their triumph with shrill cries, and in some other news, it was told they also shed tears as they apparently mourned the death of seven of their own who had been killed by a train. A police officer who was witnessing an accident, which occurred on November 15, 2001, in India's state of Assam, was quoted saying, "About a hundred elephants were circling the dead elephants that lay near the railway tracks, with tears rolling down their eyes." As Mary Beth Swan writes, a happy cry averages two minutes; a sad cry averages seven minutes.

Every human's first act shortly after being born is nothing but crying in tears. We are told by scientists that loud cry indicates the baby's lungs are functional. The neonatal studies show that thirty minutes to two hours is the average time an infant cries per day. We continue to use this voiceful, wordless, but effective strategy till our last breath in several styles as ammunition for various purposes. They are very distinguishable cries, such as attention cry, hunger cry, separation cry, pain cry, and so on. According to one research study found in *Mind Matters: A Study of Mental Health Literacy*, the average adult in the United States cries no less than three or four times a month. Between the ages of fifteen to thirty, women cry five times more frequently than men. Women's tears flow more than men's.

In the Bible, shedding tears mostly is connected to the human sorrows, griefs, sufferings, and other maladies. In our Judeo-Christian scriptures, the phrase "being in tears" is invariably a normal act of *anawim*, God's poor people of every sort. The Hebrew word *anawim* (*inwetan*) means "those who are bowed down, namely, people who are vulnerable, marginalized, and socioeconomically oppressed, and those of lowly status without earthly power, but in fact, they depend totally on their Creator for whatever they owned." These poor children of God express their hurts and pains in the form of praying in tears; they don't stop there.

At the end of every one of their tearful prayers, they include their indomitable faith and unrelenting trust and hope toward their Heavenly Parent. For example, an archetype of this sort of *anawim* prayer we hear from Jesus while he was undergoing ignominious painful final hours of his life. Mark points out at the Garden of Gethsemane Jesus was troubled and distressed acutely and his soul was sorrowful even to death, foreseeing his future crucifixion. At that moment, he prayed to his Heavenly Father, *"Abba, Father, all things are possible to you. Take this cup* [of suffering] *away from me, but not what I will but what you will"* (Mk. 14:32–36). Again while Jesus was hanging on the cross, undergoing unthinkable pain and suffering, he cried out to his Heavenly Father, *"My God, my God, why have you forsaken me?"* (Mk. 15:34). Though his Father didn't do anything about his outcry, we are told by Luke that he ended his life at the peak of his tribulation, *"Father, into your hands I commend my spirit"* (Lk. 23:46). That is the typical *anawim*'s prayer.

Jesus's prayer echoed what his Father inspired and encouraged his *anawim* people to uphold. We discover this profusely in the Books of Job and Psalms. *Anawim*, like David and Job, who were committed and intensely dedicated to their Creator as Father, Protector, and Provider, cry out to him in their moments of tribulations and trials but, amazingly, express their spirit of trust as if a weaned child to his/her parent. *"My wanderings you have noted; are my tears not stored in your flask, recorded in your book?"* (Ps. 56:9 NABRE). A Jewish community lamented in time of military defeat: *"You have fed them* [us] *the bread of tears, made them* [us] *drink tears in great measure"* (Ps. 80:6 NABRE). *"My tears have been my bread day and night, as they ask me every day, 'Where is your God?'"* (Ps. 42:3 NABRE).

God of Jesus never likes his humans shedding only tears of sorrow. But he permits it for the sake of human weakness. He let even his beloved Son Jesus weep in tears. "*When Jesus saw her weeping and the Jews who had come with her weeping, he became perturbed and deeply troubled, and said, 'Where have you laid him?' They said to him, 'Sir, come and see.' And Jesus wept. So the Jews said, 'See how he loved him'*" (Jn. 11:33–36 NABRE).

We are assured by his Word that he makes sure before our tears of sorrow dry or evaporate, we feel the spiritual joy within us. We too hear from Jeremiah the most exciting prediction of God to his people in their time of trials: "*Tears of joy will stream down their faces, and I will lead them home with great care. They will walk beside quiet streams and on smooth paths where they will not stumble. For I am Israel's father, and Ephraim is my oldest child*" (Jer. 31:9 NLT).

Tears also are generated out of the spirit with which we proceed with our ministries. It can be one of fear and trembling as Paul puts it. "*So then, my beloved, obedient as you have always been, not only when I am present but all the more now when I am absent, work out your salvation with fear and trembling*" (Phi. 2:12). As scriptural scholars explain, "fear and trembling" is a common Old Testament expression indicating awe and seriousness in the service of God.

Most of us think tears are the signs of displaying human weakness. But many spiritual writers and sages underline they are rather the icons of human dignity. Henry Ward Beecher, an American Congregationalist clergyman, social reformer, and speaker who lived in the eighteenth century, has been quoted saying, "*Tears are often the telescope by which men see far into heaven.*"

With the enlightenment received from the scriptures and tradition, any faith-filled Christian, like Paul and other disciples and saints, sheds frequently these heavenly or spiritual tears of sweet agony and those of bitter agony. The hearts of the disciples of Jesus from the day of Pentecost, the birthday of their Alma Mater, the church, have been pouring out these precious tears. It is a natural fact, as Paul indicates in his Letter to the Romans, "All creations of God await with eager expectation the revelation of the children of God; and are indeed groaning in labor pains even until now." In that same passage, Paul also underlines that we ourselves, namely, the committed disciples of Jesus, who have the first fruits of the Spirit, also groan within ourselves as we wait for adoption, the redemption of our bodies. In addition to all these natural and human tears, we read, Paul confirming amazingly, that together with the spiritually reborn humans, in the same way, the Spirit too, coming to the aid of their weakness, intercedes with inexpressible groanings (Rom. 8:18–27).

Fr. Vima Dasan (Dasan):

Undoubtedly, the tears that these disciples have been shedding are two kinds, not only generated out of bitter agony but also poured out of sweet agony. If we travel through the church history, we find this sort of double-dimensional spiritual groaning and mourning has been very common from the days of the first disciples of Jesus. In Acts, for example, we notice vividly the disciples, who were continuously with intense longing and trust (surely overwhelmed with bitter agony), stayed together in one place, silently and hopefully praying. This means going deeper into their spiritual realm, where the Spirit moved, through their in-travel religious techniques, passing through all the stations on the way as the stopovers and reaching the destiny that is nothing but the God's treasure island, where all the Spirit's gifts are buried. Once they reached there, being present intensively face-to-face with all those treasures of the Spirit—namely, wisdom, understanding, counsel, fortitude, knowledge, piety, and fear of the Lord—they began feeling powerful, fearless, and never ashamed of performing what the Spirit of truth, of love, and of peace was inspiring. At the same time, we too notice their entire personality being renewed up to the standard of Jesus: humble enough to accept their original human limitations and feeling very light as they swam either floating over the Living Waters or swimming against the current earthly waters. And what they thought they were possessing (spouses, children, properties, talents, and good names) seemed to be nothing; they would appear and smell like cow dung in front of those godly treasures. Paul describes this renewed attitude in his own flabbergasting style: "*Whatever gains I had, these I have come to consider a loss because of Christ. More than that, I even consider everything as a loss because of the supreme good of knowing Christ Jesus my Lord. For his sake I have accepted the loss of all things and I consider them so much rubbish, that I may gain Christ*" (Phi. 3:78).

The story of the disciples' tears does not end there. When they were filled with the spiritual tears of sweet agony in their reaching already the marvelous, ecstatic treasure island of God's Spirit, they also dispensed the tears of bitter agony: that, firstly, they had not yet fully coveted those treasures in themselves and, secondly, that their friends and relatives had not yet got such wonderful chance. They groan and mourn ceaselessly and beg the Lord to bestow his gifts and treasures to the whole humanity.

Dr. M. R. DeHann's definition of a tear very well sums up what I mean by the earlier scribbles: *"A tear is a distillation of the soul. It is the deepest longing of the human heart in chemical solution. It is the concentrated extract, the final precipitate of the deepest feelings of the heart, filtered through the sieve of trial and testing. True tears are not camouflage but the picture of the soul on the canvass of the emotions. They are the portraits of our deepest aspirations."*

In my experiences both as a wedding and funeral celebrant, I am accustomed to watching and even joining with my congregational gatherings in shedding tears both at the weddings and funerals of my parishioners. In weddings, we witness a blessing take place to serve and protect that new life. It is no small commitment to agree to love one other person for a lifetime. It is like being given a new life. Their witnesses are often touched by their expressions of love and devotion. It is not unusual for the blessing to be celebrated with tears of joy. Hence, shedding tears is not one of showcases of human expressions.

More than any other gesture, tears can disclose a partner's genuine feelings for the other as they read out their avowed declarations of love to each other. That makes partners relaxed and confirm themselves that they can trust each other more intensely. The same way in funeral services, the tears shed by some relatives or friends of the deceased reveal to the spectators standing around the casket their love and gratitude toward the deceased person.

Tears are, besides their physical and medical jobs to the eyes, many times act as the signs of what is hidden in the deepest level of the human spirit. This is why Antoine de Saint-Exupery very well underlined that "*it is such a secret place, the land of tears.*"

As Anne Taylor writes, "Tears release our tension in the drudgeries of day-to-day life; they make us open and vulnerable to be blessed by God and people; they strengthen the bonds between humans by operating as liaison to see each other more clearly as you truly are, beyond the surface; in addition, they bring healing to those who are divided, broken, and wounded in their relationship and giving and getting forgiveness tears settle them in peace."

People never believe that those who hold higher position in the society, especially those who are revered as saints and sages, with their rank and file, never shed tears at all. And so are the priests, being wrongly judged and set apart from human actions like shedding tears. Very surprisingly, in the Bible, as we earlier mentioned, Jesus, as a high priest, shed tears. "*In the days when he was in the flesh, he offered prayers and supplications with loud cries and tears to the one who was able to save him from death, and he was heard because of his reverence*" (Heb. 5:1–7). Priests are in no way exempted in this regard, especially that they try to lead a life committed to the values of Jesus the high priest.

From Stone Age to Age of Enlightenment and even in today's postmodern age, tear is considered to be a universal sign of sorrow, joy, and other human feelings. This is why philosophers and scientists of all ages have tried to explain shedding tears as part of a shared human language of emotional expression. Tears are universal sign, not in the sense of containing the same meaning in all times and all places. It is a universal sign because it can signify just about anything. In this book, the term *tears* is taken conveniently as the symbols of feelings of sufferings, joys, and gratitude, especially those being experienced in the lives of priests.

Fr. Dasan and Fr. Vima:

In this book, we portray the tears we shed in priestly ministry, not merely to ventilate our emotional outbursts to our friends, kith and kin, and even our so-called enemies, but most of all, to celebrate those tears as part of the blessing that has come to strengthen our union with the Lord, with the church, and certainly with our lifelong neighbors. Ultimately, this is to bring any reader of this book, especially our (international) fellow missionary priests, closer to Jesus, the One they love the most, and to the church, his beloved spouse.

The Unmatched Name(s)

Are We Missionaries or Mere International Priests?

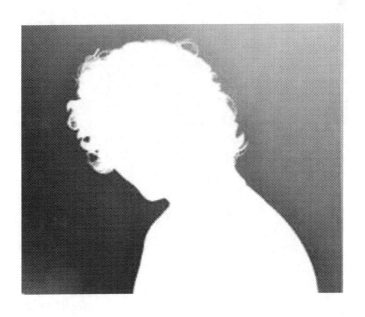

Greetings

Ben: Brother Dasan! First of all, I like to offer my best wishes and prayers as you celebrate your eightieth birthday. I am so glad you accepted my request to share your memorable experiences and priceless thoughts on the subject treated in this book.

Dasan: Thank you, Amalan, for inviting me to join you in discussing about our ministerial lives as Catholic priests. You should excuse me for calling you Amalan and not Ben, for the main reason I got used to that name from our early childhood. I hope, later in this book, you will explain how you renamed yourself.

International vs. Missionary

Ben: Certainly, I will. But before going into personal matters, let us first discuss on the core subject matter of this book. As I underlined to you, this book is entirely about our priestly ministries performed both within the confinement of the institution, within the country we had been formed and ordained, and outside of the national boundaries as the so-called international priests. Personally, I don't like to be named as international priest; rather, I prefer to be called as missionary. What do you say about it?

Every Christian Is a Missionary

Dasan: I agree with you on this matter. Every Catholic priest is none other than a missionary. First and foremost, he is missionary as every Christian goes through the sacraments of baptism and confirmation; he has been reborn and confirmed to be a missionary, meaning to be sent out to witness God in Jesus. All our church fathers and long-standing church documents repeatedly emphasize this fact, quoting the "Grand Commission" of the Lord. *"Go, therefore, and make disciples of all nations, baptizing them in the name of the Father, and of the Son, and of the Holy Spirit, teaching them to observe all that I have commanded you. And behold, I am with you always, until the end of the age."* (Matt. 28:19–20).

Ben: While you talk about Jesus's Grand Commission, I am reminded of what Pope Francis had deliberated on this issue. At a general audience, the pope, addressing the magnificent role of baptism in the transmission of the faith from generation to generation, is quoted saying, *"In effect, as from generation to generation life is transmitted, so too from generation to generation, through rebirth at the baptismal font, grace is transmitted, and by this grace the Christian People journey through time, like a river that irrigates the land and spreads God's blessing throughout the world. From the moment that Jesus gave the great commission to his disciples until today there is a chain in the transmission of the faith through Baptism. And each one of us is a link in that chain: a step forward, always; like a river that irrigates."* He too emphasized that all of us are missionary disciples, called to bring the Gospel to the world and repeated what is written in his apostolic exhortation *Evangelii Gaudium*, n. 120. *"All the baptized, whatever their position in the Church or their level of instruction in the faith, are agents of evangelization."*

Dasan: Recently I too read the final document of Aparecida, from where I am sure the pope would have gotten the spirit to insist the fact that there exists an indissoluble bond between the *mystical* and the *missionary* dimension of the Christian vocation, both rooted in baptism. "*All of us who are baptized are called to live and transmit communion with the Trinity, for evangelization is a calling to participate in the communion of the Trinity*" (n. 157). In his address to the bishops of Korea, in the Korean Episcopal Conference in Seoul, August 14, 2014, the pope was quoted saying, "*If we accept the challenge of being a missionary Church, a Church which constantly goes forth to the world and, especially, to the peripheries of contemporary society, we will need to foster that 'spiritual taste' which enables us to embrace and identify with each member of Christ's body.*" He emphasized very candidly that all church members are to be missionaries both in and outside of the church.

Ben: The challenge that the pope points out reminds me of the Lord choosing and sending his disciples for missions. In Mark's Gospel, we read the reasons he called humans to be his disciples: "*He appointed twelve whom he also named apostles that they might be with him and he might send them forth to preach and to have authority to drive out demons*" (Mk. 3:14–15).

Christian disciples are the ones who must always be with their Master, abiding in him, like vine and branches, wherever they are or whatever they do; listen to him and think with him; then separate themselves from what is dear to them and follow their Master wherever he leads. Moreover, as Mark narrates, these disciples were sent to far-off places to perform Christian works of mercy and to proclaim the Gospel of joy. "*He summoned the*

Twelve and began to send them out two by two and gave them authority over unclean spirits" (Mk. 6:7–13). In this way, Jesus emphasizes that every one of his disciples should be a missionary. Today, as then, the Christians, who for this very reason are disciples of Christ, are sent as missionaries of the merciful truth.

Dasan: Very interestingly, Amalan, we should note that Mark places the two events: of Jesus's calling and sending the disciples, immediately after his writing about the mercy of Jesus (Mk. 3:7–12), and on his experience of being rejected at Nazareth (Mk. 6:1–6). The Spirit of Jesus sends out the message to all his disciples, whom he intends to send as missionaries, that their one and only mission is bestowing mercy to the people, especially those who suffer; secondly, that they are warned about the rejection they would be encountering for being his disciples in their missionary enterprises and they should be ready to bear it with sportive spirit, as he did. Rejection is expected (Mk. 7:11): God's word is effective, but in its own way. The disciple must proclaim the message of mercy and joy and put himself on the line for it but must leave to God the results. The disciple was given a task but not guaranteed success. Certainly we both are the clear witnesses to this missionary truth that we intend to share in this book.

Priest Is a Double-Scored Missionary

Ben: Yes, brother. In addition to the common priesthood received from baptism, every priest, through his ordination, received the ministerial priesthood, which elevates him to be a double-scored missionary.

While I was studying for priesthood at St. Paul's Seminary, managed by the Jesuits of India, in Tamil Nadu, every day early morning, we would go to our seminary chapel for prayer, meditation, and Mass. During those hours, my only preoccupation was just looking up to the upper frontal portion of the sanctuary where a scriptural verse was inscribed. That verse is the golden words of St. Paul, the greatest missionary priest who ever lived and served to God. That verse is "*Segregati in Evangelium Christi.*" In English, it is translated as "Set apart for the Gospel of Christ." "*Paul, a slave of Christ Jesus, called to be an apostle and set apart for the gospel of God*" (Rom. 1:1). The Jesuit founders had chosen these words as the motto of the seminary. That motto sparked in my heart and mind the missionary spirit, and it continues burning still in my inner sanctuary. A priest, in whatever situation he has been called from or for whatever purpose he has selected this priesthood, has been, once and for all, segregated from the world, from all other earthly clingings and holdings, only for proclaiming Christ's Gospel. Without being sent by Christ, I was convinced it was impossible for me to be segregated from my secular-life milieu. I am, therefore, so convinced that every priest ordained in the church, in any corner of the world, is to be named a missionary. Please bear with me as I want to read to you a few passages relevant to this sort of conviction, from the documents of Second Vatican Council, which has been in the formation and ministries of postmodern priests like you and me. These would assist in our conversation regarding our priestly ministries.

Dasan: OK, go ahead. I too will add some of them.

Ben: The Second Vatican Council, in its Decree on the Priesthood, or *Presbyterorum Ordinis*, no. 10, splendidly has declared, "*The spiritual gift which priests receive at their ordination prepared them not for a sort of limited and narrow mission but for the widest possible and universal mission of salvation 'even to the ends of the earth' (Acts 1:8), for every priestly ministry shares in the universality of the mission entrusted by Christ to his apostles. The priesthood of Christ, in which all priests really share, is necessarily intended for all peoples and all times, and it knows no limits of blood, nationality or time, since it is already mysteriously prefigured in the person of Melchisedech. Let priests remember, therefore, that the care of all churches must be their intimate concern.*"

Dasan: In this context, Amalan, conciliar fathers, considering the very serious dearth of priests, which is hindering the evangelization of many areas, instructed all the bishops around the globe to "*send some of their better priests, who offer themselves for mission work and have received a suitable preparation, to those dioceses which are lacking in clergy, where at least for a time they will exercise their missionary ministry in a spirit of service.*"

Priests of Vatican II New Age Church

Ben: I noticed how the church of twenty-first century, where we belong to, is so much concerned about her missionary duty and encourages all her priests, especially of those dioceses that are blooming with vocations to the priesthood. I read in her document a detailed demand proposed to the priests: "*The priests of such dioceses as are rich in vocations should show themselves willing and ready, with the permission of their own ordinaries (bishops), to volunteer for work in other regions, missions or endeavors which are poor in numbers of clergy.*" I, as a priest of the Vatican II New Age Church, was so much influenced by such innovative but necessary strategy of the church. I am sure you too would have felt the same.

Dasan: Absolutely. I remember I had a personal conversation with you in 1986 revealing to you my problem of coping with my ministries in institutions. I told you that I hate to become an institutionalized priest, whereas I am of the charismatic personality, in the sense, I am more of being a missionary to be moving, to be serving different kinds of people. I too explained to you how I was encouraged by some of the Vatican II writings, especially on the missionary character and ministry of the church and her priesthood. The verse you quoted earlier holds good not only for diocesan priests like you but also more for the religious priests like me.

Ben: Thank you for reminding me of that conversation between us. May be, that sharing of yours would have been sowing some seed in my heart too and as I was so much interested to put into practice, as well as in my communication ministries writing, composing, preaching, teaching, etc., I read and reread those writings on the church's missionary spirit and ministry. Today if I am what I am in the United States thanks to those days of meditating and reflecting the words of the church based on scriptures and traditions, surely the signs of the time.

The Glorious Missionary Heritage

Dasan: Now I clearly understand why you prefer the term *missionary* to *international*. Anyone who has stepped out of his/her own native, personal, linguistic, cultural territories, boundaries, and likings for the sake of the Gospel, in the name of the church, is supposed to be a missionary in its right sense.

Ben: Unfortunately, many Catholics in America (I am sure in Europe too) are still not ready to accept that those priests who came to their churches from other parts of the globe are truly missionaries sent by God through Jesus to them. I asked some of my American friends on this issue. They simply said, "We know you are a Catholic priest. That's enough for us. The rest of its knottiest descriptions is overall the concern of the clergy." They were very plain in their response, but it saddened me very much to discover how even ordinary Catholics have lost sight of the glorious heritage of the church's missionary tradition regarding her priests. Catholics of postmodern age found it hard to digest that the church still has the duty to send priests all over the world to be her missionaries only to spread the Gospel of joy wherever the social and cultural environment demands as the signs of the time.

Dasan: Amalan, we should not blame only laypeople in this matter. There are certain flaws among us priests in handling this missionary duty. First, we have to confess that most of the priests moving from one country to another or one state to another keep certain personal agenda behind, namely, our own personal gratification. I mean getting a better life with convenience and comfort as much as possible or simply running away from hardships they had been enduring while they were serving in their local congregation or the diocese. Consequently, our missionary spirit has fled away from our priestly hearts, and all that we perform or accomplish in a new environment turn out to be either fake, useless, neither cold nor hot, and even poisonous.

Ben: I don't disagree with you in this matter. I come to a conclusion that it may be the reason for many, especially our priests, to think of us only as "international" priests, indicating that we are like— forgive me for my usual crazy usage—some sort of *supply-and-demand commodities* in this secular global economy of salvation! In addition to the twitted ministries of the so-called international priests, as some of my fellow missionaries and even a few bishops finger-point, there is some kind of wounded-pride syndrome pervading and frightening among the traditional and even modern Catholics. What I mean is this: Centuries ago, even now, priests and nuns from different parts of the Europe, where undoubtedly our Catholic Church was baptized and bred (you know well the birthplace of Christianity is not Europe, rather it was the Middle East, Palestine, which is historically the native abode of Jesus, Mary, and Joseph) by our church fathers, popes, and theologians and majority of canonized saints. Countries like France, Italy, Spain, Portugal, and Ireland and so on had been graced and blessed by the Good Missionary, Jesus Christ, who sent many of his followers to all corners of the world to bring the message of the Gospel.

Dasan: We are indeed proud to be called not only as Thomas Christians but also the converts of hundreds of European missionaries who founded, in the name of the universal church, the following missions: French Mission, Spanish Mission, Irish Mission, etc. Here I should thankfully acknowledge the Jesuit missionaries' tireless and breathtaking endeavors in our native place, I mean in our native village. Actually, the Catholic parishes and institutions at that time in the state of Tamil Nadu, then was called Madras, were founded largely by two missions: French and Spanish. Our native parish, St. Michael's, belonged to the French Mission. Hence, many French Jesuit missionaries played a major role in its development, mainly religious and educational levels. I know personally the dedication of those missionaries in learning our culture and language and accommodating to our age-old customs, which sometimes appeared uncouth. They really loved us from the bottom of their hearts and expressed it very clearly, "They loved us because we are the children of God." In a way, they were my role models and fire-blazing inspiration to choose my future lifestyle.

Ben: Well said, my brother. When they were such wonderful priests, they had their own personal weaknesses as any other human beings. They had their own downfalls and failures. Our people, as I noticed when I was growing in the same atmosphere, never bothered about the failures of these missionaries;

rather, they offered the same respect and love toward their foreign priests. I was dumbfounded to notice such naive attitude from my elders. Since I was a little kid, I couldn't ask anything about it. Later when I became an adolescent, I was bold enough to ask some of my village elders the reason for such complacent reaction toward their missionaries. You know what they said to me? With open mind, in a plain-speaking style of any rural Indian, they told me, *"My dear boy! These priests were sent by God from heaven. They are like God's Son, Jesus. They are truly angels. Even if they fail in certain things, we should never say anything evil against them. Rather, we should silently and willingly accept them and do what they order us to do. Otherwise, God would punish us."*

Oh my god! Are these people cranky? I thought. *Are they simpletons? Why should they pour out such respect and admiration to them?* I shared this with one of my colleagues later in the seminary.

He said in a sarcastic and jovial way, "Maybe these missionaries' skin is white. As any other members of color-bound social systems, since your villagers are dark-complexioned, they would have esteemed these missionaries as godsent angels straight from heaven! They were literally color-blind!"

In Sincere Search of Genuine Titles

Dasan: I foresee now what you are driving at. You feel that the priests with whom we have joined as international or missionary priests feel their pride has been damaged and hurt because of our arrival; secondly, you sense that these people whom we serve are more color-bound than Christ-oriented. Am I correct?

Ben: That is completely right. Our priest friends, among whom we serve, never want us to be esteemed as missionaries. It belittles their traditional image and spoils their entire monolithic understanding of the centuries-old fact that "*we are the church. We only can bring the message of the Gospel to the world. Only we possess the spiritual and religious stamina to go out and preach to the entire world, except we ourselves and all others, particularly in the so-called third world, are still pagans and, very sadly, barbarians. Therefore, how can some priests coming all the way from those dark places serve here in our midst as missionaries? They can be only a sack of 'supply' priests.*" Thus, there is an identity crisis nagging and, in many places, hurting the "faith of the unfaithful" in the church of today.

Dasan: That was my experience too, which I will discuss with you later. But, Amalan! Before we blame the prejudices we the international priests face, we must acknowledge how the church in the Western world coined the word *international* to differentiate us from local priests. First of all, they didn't like us to be called foreign priests. Naming us "foreign" would have been felt by them as crude and uncivilized in the unified and holy church milieu. They too didn't proclaim to their congregations that we are from different countries and, thus, identified as Indian, Chinese, Vietnamese, Nigerian, Mexican, Sri Lankan, Filipino, and so on. Rather, the first person who tried to search for some fitting term would have thought it better to name us as international and solve the negative problems. Also, this term would have been esteemed as very close to our church's primary characteristic, Catholic, meaning universal.

Ben: You are right. I can add one more view on this matter. In this postmodern age, a new trend is empowering all, particularly artists and musicians like me. We have been composing many musical pieces in line with our local and traditional culture and musical styles. Now due to the modern, innovative technology and science, we want to go a little further and compose music that can cover the whole global market. We name that music style as world music, or global music, which is nothing but the blending of all styles of music around the world and all kinds of instruments used in various parts of the world. Music, thus, becomes universal as the Catholic Church. The same way we the missionaries may be called world priests, as one school of theology in the USA uses in an online ads for their training sessions offered to these international priests. Thank God it does not describe them as worldly priests. Haha.

Be Careful What You Coin

Dasan: When you say "worldly priests," I am reminded of the wrong view held by some religious priests like me about you diocesan priests when you are identified as secular in order to differentiate you from the religious. Thinking in that line, I too advised you while you were in the seminary not to be worldly. Against such biased opinion, I still remember, how you retorted to me. After you were ordained and sent to perform your first ministry in a poverty-stricken area, you wrote me, describing the hardships you underwent during those years of parochial life, and in a funny way, you added, "Brother, you the religious make vows, but we the secular observe them."

Ben: I am sorry for such joke. It is only a half-baked interpretation of priestly life. Every priest has his own ups and downs, and the tears that we discuss in this book are shed invariably by every priest—either religious or diocesan. Let us go back to our conversation on the titles. As many in the USA feel the term *international* does not fully cover our identity and ministry, they try their best to coin some more. One among them (I noticed in one of the online advertisements of a school of theology that I mentioned earlier) uses a new term, "mission priests." This is about workshops on *language*, *culture*, and *ministry*, mainly for international priests, conducted at Saint Meinrad Seminary and School of Theology. Advertising one of those workshops, *Zenit*, a Rome-based online news agency, wrote as its title: "Accent Training and Acculturation Workshops for Recently Arrived Mission Priests." That is how people give a second title about the priests who come here to perform their priestly ministry. I think many of our church members fail in their recognition of the right status of these priests with an attitude of profiling as some persons from mission land. In other words, they mean, "they are lower than us, as we are the ones who take Christianity and its faith to other countries and languages." Is it the right and just way? It all comes out of wounded pride and lack of true Christian spirit. Those days are gone in the wind and, in many cases, as the heavenly tornado effect of changing the face of not only of the earth but, primarily, that of his church. My heart pleads in front of them: Let us stop dividing the world as our ancestors, I mean recent ones, who wrongly did; they fooled themselves and others by measuring the people by mere economic status, racial affluence, and religious aristocracy.

Dasan: I browsed all the responses you got from the international priest friends working in the USA. Everyone admits they should be called missionaries and not by any other term.

Mission in Multiple Colors

Ben: Even when they are incardinated to the local dioceses, where they came to serve like me, they must be considered missionaries till their death. This term should be one of prestigious titles the church should preserve as her revealed and beloved heritage. Undoubtedly, every Christian, and certainly every priest, is a missionary, as we pointed out. In this postmodern age, not only the world we live in is full of non-Christians, but also such people are there in our church. Pope Francis insisted this point, in an audience (3-6-15) with the Neocatechumenal Community *missio ad gentes* families, explaining about its call to support their mission in life. He said, *"You will go in Christ's name to the whole world to bring his Gospel: Christ precedes you, Christ accompanies you, Christ will bring to fulfillment the salvation of which you are bearers!"* The pope also described who these non-Christians are. He categorized them in three groups: *"those who have never heard or speak of Jesus Christ; those who have forgotten who Jesus Christ was, who Jesus Christ* is; *those who are baptized but who, because of the influence of secularization, worldliness, and many other things, have forgotten the faith.* He advised, "Awaken that faith!" That is what the church's mission is all about. While all of Christ's disciples perform mission works as their primary religious duty, we international priests, who have been pushed out by the Divine—whatever may be its origin, background, and its process—we have been set apart in the middle of our priestly life to go out to the other side of the globe to fulfill the Great Commission of Jesus and become a pattern, a role model, or an inspiration to all other disciples of the same Master.

Be Prepared and Be Qualified

Dasan: Well said, Amalan. A priest who is fully engaged in this sort of modern mission work is expected of fulfilling some requirements and be qualified for such awesome work. Our pope Francis reiterated many times this truth whenever he met priests, bishops, and professors and students of different seminaries. Let me read to you what he said when he addressed the professors and students of the diocesan seminary of Rome, the "Almo Collegio Capranica"(1-20-12): *"'Formation for the priesthood likewise requires integrity, maturity, asceticism, constancy and heroic fidelity in all aspects. All this must be founded upon a solid spiritual life animated by an intense relationship with God, as individuals and in the community, with a particular care for liturgical celebrations and frequent recourse to the Sacraments. Priestly life requires an ever-increasing thirst for sanctity, a clear 'sensus Ecclesiae' and an openness to fraternity without exclusion or bias,' said the Holy Father.*

"Always maintain a profound sense of the history and traditions of the Church,' the Pope told his audience. 'Here you have the opportunity to open yourselves to an international horizon. Learn to understand the situations of the various countries and Churches of the world. Ready yourselves to approach all the men and women you will meet, ensuring that no culture is a barrier to the Word of life, which you must announce even with your lives.

"'The Church expects a lot from young priests in the work of evangelization and new evangelization. I encourage you in your daily efforts that, rooted in the beauty of authentic tradition and profoundly united to Christ, you may bring Him into your communities with truth and joy.'"

The Tears of Gratitude

*I will lavish choice portions
on the priests.*

—Jer. 31:14

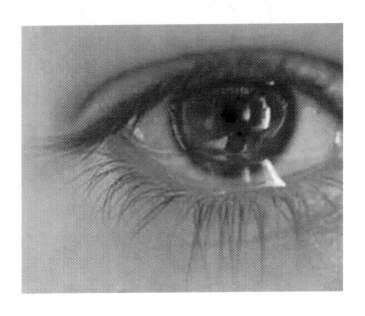

Grateful for "Starting Troubles"

Ben: Brother! Would you please describe your childhood days at home and how you were introduced to vocation to the priesthood!

Dasan: I am grateful to God for the good and pious Catholic family into which I was born, a family that was not very rich, yet we were not poor, and we never starved for food; even in famine times, our parents secured enough for food.

Our dad was a rigid, strict, and severe man when it came to moral life. Once he tied me to a post and beat me for smoking cigarette. Early morning at five, he would wake me up to go with him for parish Mass. If I had done some mischief and if our mother had reported it to him, I would not be given night meal. If I came late for family night prayer, I would be kept kneeling for the rest of the prayer time. Every evening, he would take me with him to the grotto for parish community prayer and would insist that I said three Hail Marys for my becoming a priest one day. For all these spiritual upbringings, I am very grateful to my father and to my God.

Though strict and severe, our dad was extremely kind to me. Most of the days, I used to carry lunch for him to some distant village where he was a teacher. After he finished eating his meal, he always kept aside a portion of the meal for me to eat. At night when I was sleeping, he would sit near me to fan me, driving away flies and mosquitoes. When I felt going out to answer call of nature, he would accompany me across the field, for I was afraid of the dark.

After I finished elementary school at my native village, my family took to Madurai Town to put me in the apostolic school run by Jesuit fathers, hoping that one day I would become a Jesuit priest. But since there was no place in that school due to my oldest brother's pleas, the rector admitted me to high school boarding. As I was studying there, my oldest brother used to visit me often and to meet the headmaster to inquire how I was faring in studies. Once when I was playing hockey, I got hit by a ball in the leg, and it got swollen. The doctor had to operate on me, and my mother came rushing from the village and sat by me till the operation was over.

I passed high school and was preparing to join the Society of Jesus. Before leaving, I had still to pay arears to boarding fees. My oldest brother came again to appeal to the rector to wave the balance, which he did and went to my village, and a letter came from Jesuit Provincial asking me to come to the novitiate on a particular date. But unfortunately, I fell seriously ill with typhoid. It took one month for me to recover from fever. During that one month, my whole family showered on me love and attention, which made me feel that my whole family wanted me to somehow go to the novitiate and join the society for priesthood. Finally, my brother-in-law took me to the novitiate, and both of us arrived in a horse-driven cart (*judka*). I do not know how to thank my family for all they did to enable me to reach this stage of life. I thanked God with tears that night.

Ben: That is very revealing to me what you shared about your childhood memories. I know you are ready to know more about my childhood experiences and how I got into the priestly field.

Dasan: Yes, Amalan. I want to hear it from you, mainly because I didn't stay with you long when you were in elementary. Remember, while you were at sixth grade, I already joined the Jesuit novitiate. I too know how you were taken into the dream of becoming a priest. It was our dad, as he did to me, who should have been the primary initiator for your choosing the priestly vocation, wasn't he?

Ben: You are 100 percent right, brother! Let me explain to you what sort of "starting troubles" I encountered at home and how I am grateful for them all.

First of all, I am grateful as you are for being born in India, despite its social, political, and environmental grimy situation. The whole world is aware of the mystic environment of India, the subcontinent whose greatness consists of maintaining its ideology of syncretism living through in its thick and thin over the centuries. What Patrick Smith, a columnist, praising this remarkable "Indianness," wrote once in the *Fiscal Times* defined it well in a popular style: "*It is a salad of cultures, traditions, faiths, languages, and what have you blended into the unique thing called 'Indianness.'*" I am grateful to be born in such rare-blend milieu.

I have to confess here that being born as the baby of the family, I was truly a spoiled brat. That is in many ways.

Positively, our mom loved me so much that she poured her abundant love on me and I never, not even a single moment, suffer from life's hardships, like hunger, thirst, or even joining with the elders in their physical labors of sweating and bleeding. She was always my "bodyguard," while our dad was my "soul guard." My mom's manner of protecting me was sometimes too extreme; even as a child, I disliked and disapproved it. For example, she never wanted me to be alone when we would go to our nearby lake for bathing. Actually, in that lake, there were two separate locations—one for men and boys and the other for women and girls. When she took me to that lake, she never allowed me to join the boys; instead, she kept me near her along with women and girls. Many times my friends giggled about my girlishness. I too began disliking such exclusive motherly protection.

Our dad—as he did to you but little more acutely, because he knew I was a spoiled brat, because of his dutiful consciousness of safeguarding my childhood soul and of realizing his dream of making me a priest—was very much concerned about my completion of daily religious rituals and compelling me follow every bit of the moral principles he had in his spiritual or religious storage. Whereas my personality was overwhelmed with artistic interests and freedom and love-based walk of life, our dad, I think, tried his best decoding my original self by thrusting me into the Catholic puritanical and unquestioning moral and religious one. In later days, I, with a little cynicism, called it the brainwashing.

However, I tell you, once I was of age in my rebirthed life in Jesus, I felt all those troubles I underwent were the source and foundation of my priestly ministry. I am grateful for those troubles.

With the love of our mother and by the orthodox faith and Christian discipline of our dad, I was brought up and made to grow in all aspects of Catholic Christian life. It is true I didn't like the way our dad thrust his ambition into my life. Because of his committed promise to the Lord, I felt as if I was pushed hard into the ministry of priesthood in the Catholic Church. After my completion of elementary education at my village church school, as it was done to you, I was taken to Madurai Town, twenty-five miles away from the native village. Since at that time, there were no proper public transportations from our village to Madurai Town, except one train that ran twice a week, and that too had its stop station four miles away from the village. We had to wake up early morning and fast enough to reach the station. So to us, the journey to Madurai was like going overseas. Being the baby of my family and being attached very close to my mother, I first found it hard to leave her and her environment. Till this day, my inner heart beats me to death with those nightmares of being thrown into a shelter like an orphan. You don't know how much I was crying every day while I was studying in Madurai.

One of the games God played with me was that I got the seat in the apostolic school and you didn't. It was a petit seminary run by the Society of Jesus, mostly meant to recruit boys after their high school studies to their congregation. While I was so sorry being alone without Mom, I felt happy thinking a little bit I could be free of our dad's enforcement of discipline. But I tell you, the disciplining rod continues to chasten me in the forms of Jesuit directors.

Meanwhile, I found some way to express my artistic talents and inner ambitions of becoming popular. Though I was not recruited into the boys' choir to sing inside the church, I became a popular singer of film songs among my peers. Moreover, I was offered chances to act in the high school anniversary dramas. That too made me popular, and many teachers liked me.

There was one strange thing happening in my inner sanctuary. Our directors occasionally brought some vocation promoters of different congregations to address us. I tell you, in every session, I was burning with fire; I thought I must be something greater, better than what I was. I started praying on my own accord, never in compulsion. But still my heart was aching to join my mom and family.

Here I have to testify how the compassionate fatherhood of God can come down to help a young man like me who has been spoiled, very naive, and formed as a fear-cast chicken and incapacitated to take freely a choice of my own. I don't say he came in my dreams or offered some indescribable visions; rather, he used some selected humans to elevate and strengthen my inner vitality to go beyond. Yes, consciously or unconsciously, I am driven by an impulse to go out of my blues, to go beyond the negative situations I had been pushed into by the family, the community, and surely the religion. This pulling and pushing continues till this day. Later I can explain to you more on this.

Dasan: Amalan! I am really surprised to hear all the turbulences you went through in your childhood. I too had such negative feelings about how our dad dealt with our childhood and how he behaved adamantly in order to realize his one and only ambition, namely, we both must, by all means, become priests of God. As you underlined, I have forgiven our dad—much more, I began appreciating all that he did to us as blessings in disguise. Now tell me when and why you changed your name.

Ben: It is a long story, but let me give you a brief exposition of it. You know my baptismal name was Amalorpavam Vima. Our dad was a staunch devotee of Mary, and as explained about his dream and pledge of making two of his sons, you and me, he named us after two names of Mary as a symbol of dedicating us to her protection and support. He gave you the name Viagula Dasan, which, in Sanskrit, means "the servant of the Sorrowful Mother," and to me, the name Amalorpavam, which is a Sanskrit term meaning, literally, "immaculate conception." While your name has at least a male reference (*Dasan*, servant), mine was entirely a female name, usually given to girls. In my youth, I was sad about this, mostly because I became popular in the public with my music compositions and other arts. So while I was in the seminary, unofficially but artistically, I gave to myself a male version for my name: Amalan Vima, which mostly denotes "Jesus, born without sin." From then on, I came to be known in that name among all my friends, superiors, and relatives living in South India and all my Tamil well-wishers around the globe.

When I came as missionary to America and decided to live the rest of my life and die among my American friends and the Spirit moved me very urgently to play low key in all my ministries for the Lord and stop fretting over to covet a good name in public as well as melt down my spirit as humbly as possible to get all blessings from God and share with my American friends, I decided to become as little as I can and as last and unknown in the human crowd. There emerged a biblical name in my mind one day while I was praying: Benjamin, the baby of Jacob, the last one among his sons. Besides, it aptly kept me to my roots of being born as a baby in our family of eight. When I became naturalized, I was officially named as Benjamin A. Vima, which I thought was a kind of second baptism in the Spirit. Thus, I joined the unknown crowd of immigrant dreamers in America.

Dasan: I am overwhelmed with excitement hearing how God let you to play his cards in his missionary game. Now explain to me about the sources that assisted you in making priestly vocation as your life's commitment during the early years of priestly formation.

Grateful for Mentors

Ben: In the vocation process of my priestly life, undoubtedly, the fear of God that had been instilled in me by my dad has been the number 1 source, especially in avoiding all occasions of sins, and consequently, I escaped from becoming a perverted young man, as some of my peers had been. Though I didn't know the reality of priestly life and even my inner spoiled self hated to proceed in this vocation journey, that kind of godly fear overpowered me.

Secondly, religiously and spiritually speaking, I am sure Mother Mary had been a heavenly protector and builder of my vocation. As our dad made it for both of us a compulsory habit in our lives, I was always praying three Hail Marys daily to her before going to bed for protecting me and keeping me in this traveling to the unknown island.

Thirdly, the preachers from different congregations who often addressed us from our days in the apostolic school Madurai and the authors of spiritual books and the lives of saints who propelled me to go forward even though my young heart was broken and bruised by many unwanted and unprecedented events activated by other human beings but with goodwill and love.

The fourth one is none other than you, Dasan. If I miss to add you in this list, I am an ungrateful brat. First of all, you had been my inspiration to enter into this priestly vocation. Though you were eleven years older than I and very early in my boyhood you accepted the call of God to become one of St. Ignatius's sons, your personal presence and surely absence too feel the height and weight of this call. In addition, the good you have done to me and to my priestly life by your frequent mails (at that time, there were no modern communication gadgets), writing to me while I was undergoing priestly formation.

Dasan: Thanks, Amalan, for including me in the team of your vocation catalysts. As you underlined, we both as young boys walked in troubled waters mostly caused by our elders. But later when we came to a spot where our God hooked us very strongly and intimately, we were enlightened to say, "Thank you, God, for letting us safely through the starting troubles." And we too are grateful for our respectful elders for leading us on the right track, as the Star of the East did to the magi, toward our life goal, which our Creator had already designed for both of us.

Grateful for Priestly Formation

Ben: I know that you were not given a place in the apostolic school but continued your high school studies staying at St. Mary's boarding school. You should have been very much hurt by losing the chance to stay in an environment that developed a sense of vocation, as it did it to me. Now tell me how did you get into the liking of Jesuits and entered into their novitiate?

Dasan: When the time came to leave home to study for priesthood, my parish priest, Father Kurien, SJ, was the moving force who was regularly instilling into me the desire to join the society. His prayer life touched me. He showed me great love at his meals. I used to fan him at his meals like a child fans his father. Weekly he used to hear my confessions with other schoolboys. I used to serve at his Latin Mass although I did not understand Latin. My parish priest was so kind, but when he got angry, no one could stand in front of him. But he never scolded me. He had a soft heart for me, thus drawing me to religious life.

Once his sister-in-law came from Kerala to visit him. Though an angry man by nature, he showed great family affection to her. Once some Catholic priests belonging to Syro-Malankara rite came to our parish and said Mass, a long Mass, with long prayers. Parishioners smiled and giggled, but Father Kurien treated them with great respect and affection. My parish priest used to travel to nearby substations by bull-o-cart to say Sunday masses. Sometime he used to take me with him in the cart. Thus, my parish priest inspired me to join the society. His prayer life, his masses, his love and affection for me, his anger at injustices and lies, and his dedication to his parishioners all attracted me to the religious order the Society of Jesus, to which he belonged. Once there was fire in my village, houses in front of my own house were burning. The parish bell wrong. Soon my parish priest rushed to the spot, knelt down before the burning houses, and prayed to God for help. Often I used to see him carrying Eucharist to sick people when I, with the rest of my family, knelt to adore the Eucharist Lord. These unforgettable events increased my desire to join the Society of Jesus.

Another foreign missionary who inspired me to join the Society of Jesus was Father Wenish, SJ. He used to give long sermons to my parishioners using huge pictures. He used to take me privately to his room and showed me small vestments that he as a boy at his own home wore while role-playing Mass. It was he, when I finished elementary school, who took me walking and by train to St. Mary's school in Madurai and recommended me to the apostolic school director and asked him to send me to the Jesuit novitiate in Dindigul. There were other two priests, Fathers. Loze, SJ, and Moran, SJ, who used to come to our village to learn Tamil. As I taught them my language, they, in turn, taught me Latin. They too, with their spiritual sharing with me and explanation on the Society of Jesus, inspired me join the Society of Jesus. I am sincerely grateful to all these wonderful and dedicated Jesuits.

Ben: As both of us agree, it was our dad who had ignited in our young hearts the fire of vocation to priestly life. I am certain you too will agree with me that our mom would have never desired to send us away from her. This I heard from her own mouth before she passed away in her hundreds. I got this answer from her by my frequent bitter questioning of the parental compulsion that made me make such unrelished choice of going to the seminary. She, in tears, told me that it was our dad's plan and not her choice and that she tried her best to dissuade her husband from sending us to become priests. She added she couldn't stop him but, finally, accepted his decision because he revealed to her that he had already made a vow to God to dedicate two of his sons to serve him as his priests. However, our mother had a unique place in our passing through the initial situation of "starting troubles" by her loving gestures of healing and encouraging. She even sent loving, consoling, and advising letters to me (since she didn't go to school and didn't know reading and writing, she must have gotten help from some of my village students or fellow teachers), even hiding some rupees inside the envelopes for my pocket money. In one letter, she said that she was sorry she couldn't do much help in our priestly life, but she assured that she was reciting the rosary to Mary daily for both of us. I know very well she did this till her last breath.

One more important thing I have to add here. As I was the baby of the family and since she knew that as religious priest, you would be away from our region, she wanted to see me stay closer to her. So when I completed my high school studies, again I was unable to decide which kind of priestly life I should choose, religious or diocesan. I turned to our parents for support as a weaning child. While our dad was not concerned about that (his only concern was I must become priest by all means), our mother stood there and categorically advised me to become a diocesan priest. This is because she thought if I become a diocesan priest, at least I would be closer to her than you were as religious. Unfortunately, I am sorry I disappointed her. Actually, more than you, I was far away from her because of my ambitious life goal of "going always beyond."

Dasan: Although we were studying for the same priesthood, we hardly met each other at home except when we came home for brief vacation. Isn't that right? When you were studying in elementary school in our native village, I remember I was often scolded for not doing his studies properly and for other small mischiefs because like our dad, I too was very fond of you for various reasons: you were the youngest "baby" in our family, and I wanted you to become priest, and for other reasons.

When our dad decided to send you to priesthood, I wanted you join me in the Society of Jesus so that you could always be with me. At one family meal when our dad asked you about it, you declined but were ready to become a diocesan priest. I thought the main reason for this was, seeing me so rigid and you a hilarious, histrionic individual, it did not have any attraction to my way of life. Now after listening to you how you were totally Mama's baby, I changed my consideration. Though I was sad that you did not join the society, I was very happy that you were willing to become a priest, though a diocesan.

Ben: Now tell me about those years of your Jesuit formation.

Dasan: At the novitiate when I met the novice master, I asked him innocently and playfully why he rejected me from the apostolic school, and I also added, "I am here to become a Jesuit, whereas the boy you took into apostolic school has gone to become diocesan seminarian!" He smiled and said, "That is how the will of God works." And that was the first lesson I learned in the novitiate! I am grateful to God for this lesson.

The two years of my living in the novitiate was a time of great joy. It was the time I laid a strong spiritual foundation. The long and short retreats I made touched me so deeply that I can say it now, if I am still a Jesuit, it was due to the impact the long retreat made on me. I enjoyed reading the lives of the Jesuit saints. They aroused in me a great desire to become like them. The rigorous spiritual training I got from my father at home helped me a lot to go through the discipline and spiritual exercises joyfully. They transformed me so much that whenever I visited my family, my father used to ask me why I did not talk and smile and laugh as I used to when I was a boy at home. I just smiled.

After I took my first vows, I was sent to Kodaikanal Hills for juniorate. I learned some languages and rhetoric for two years. I loved the hills: its forests and tall trees. I enjoyed sitting under the trees, meditating and praying. I enjoyed long walks; it was in the hills I began the custom of long evening walks, a practice I kept up for years and years. I am grateful to God for giving me good health because of such long and nonstop walks.

There is a chapel on the top of that hill dedicated to our Lady of Lazarette. I used to walk to the chapel often to sit and pray to our Lady, begging her to do well in my studies and make me a good Jesuit priest and to fill me with knowledge and wisdom.

After my juniorate, I was sent down to the plains. I was put in charge of prefecting schoolboys in the boarding. I was strict and kind with the boys, the qualities I carried with me from my father at home. Wherever I was posted, I was selected to read at the table for the fathers at the table. All liked my voice and articulation and clarity. The fathers' appreciation gave me moral boost. I was thus privileged to be chosen as a special reader for the elite group of fathers.

Ben: I am sure all these paved the way for you to be sent to college for higher studies, especially to specialize in Tamil language and literature.

Dasan: Absolutely. For all this, I am grateful to my Jesuit superiors, who began to think I was fit enough for higher studies. This gave me great joy and enthusiasm to excel in Tamil language, spoken and written as well.

As I was going through Tamil studies, I began writing and speaking attractive and beautiful Tamil, which won the appreciation and admiration of all. I was in great demand to preach all over Tamil Nadu after my ordination. Wherever I preached, people crowded just to listen to my Tamil speeches and sermons. As I saw the crowds of faithful in front of me, my own faith deepened. In fact, religious crowds kept my faith and my vocation to priesthood intact. I was inspired to see the crowd of the faithful, and it burnt within me the fire of the Spirit.

Ben: I too have vivid memory of attending some of your sermons preached to large gatherings of our Catholics. On many occasions at the end of your homilies, the faithful clapped their hands in appreciation of your religious oratory! I was very proud of you, and I too was inspired to be one of that kind of preacher one day.

Dasan: What about your life journey from seminary to parish ministry in your diocese?

Ben: Brother! As I have revealed earlier, my mind was always in troubled waters due to the starting troubles I personally experienced in my choice of vocation. Such tension and negative thoughts kept nagging at me, and I was not fully concentrating on my philosophical studies and spiritual exercises in the first three years in the major seminary. I tried my best and worst to cope with my inner struggles by distracting myself with all kinds of extracurricular activities of music, drama, and outward social ministries.

Dasan: I am really grateful to God that I had a role to play in your formation toward priesthood. When you were in the seminary, I was hearing from your professors, as they were Jesuits, that you began to reveal your histrionic talents, such as singing, stage acting, writing and directing dramas, and becoming the number 1 soloist in the seminary choir. I too was told that you were so immersed in music that your superiors suspected that you were diverting your attention and were distracted from your main studies in philosophy and from spiritual exercises.

One day your rector phoned to me and said, "Dasan, I am concerned for your brother, Amalan." This rector was our family friend, and he was a dear friend to me, personally, because I taught him Tamil whenever he used to come to our village for his holidays. He continued, "The whole seminary admires him for his artistic talents, but I feel sad to say he is not faring well in his priestly studies. Therefore, I have decided to send him away from the seminary. What do you say?"

I was jolted; my father would certainly weep. Then I took courage and said to the rector, "Father, do not send him away from the seminary. Instead, send him for one or two years of regency in a surrounding parish, and then you can take him back into the seminary." Fortunately, rector yielded to my suggestion.

Ben: Let me say how I coped with the regency. When this plan of one-year regency was proposed to me, I was shocked and moved to tears. The main issue in this matter was that I felt ashamed to be separated from my class members, who would be soon elevated to the first step to priestly life and starting soon their theological studies. I too thought I was betrayed by my superiors, to whom I was very candid and spontaneous in revealing my inner turmoil and tension going on regarding my self-imposed vocation. I never thought I would be treated that way because of my childish behavior.

When I went home that summer, the whole family was in distress; however, while our dad and mom were grieving about my future and couldn't make another plan of action for me, our married siblings encouraged me to discontinue the seminary life, and they promised support to send me to a teachers' training school. I was very much perplexed in deciding my future to continue or discontinue my pursuit of priestly life. I wanted your input in this regard. But you were still in your priestly formation course and living far away (Pune, North India) from our village; we could contact only by letters. Thank God, you wrote wonderful letters both to me and to our parents and expressed his concern about my future but advising our parents to let me choose my own path, and you too advised me about the pros and cons of this one-year break offered to me by the Lord and suggested to me I take this bitter break for the sake of God. You assured that God would elevate me to the high peak of his love. You also exhorted me that I should try this one-year life in a parish and if nothing worked out, then all of us would agree that it was the will of God that I drop from the vocation to priestly life. I tell you honestly that I was grateful to God, for the first time in my life, I was offered a chance to decide about my future of my own accord. Smilingly then, I went to a rural parish my local bishop chose for me.

Dasan: I knew, Amalan, how hard it must have been for you to bear the insult and shame of being sent out as some sort of punishment. But I tell you how much I was grateful to God that you chose that bitter regency and how you were determined to become priest though you paid a heavy stake. Our family and I were so happy to hear from our neighbors how you won the hearts and minds of your parish priest and parishioners with your obedient and docile services to them and through your multiple artistic talents used in and out of the churches.

Ben: Undoubtedly, while I was doing my regency program in that rural parish, as a young, sociable, and talented seminarian, I attracted all the Catholics, even in and around that region. And my services and undertakings in simplicity and docility pleased the parish priest, and at the end of the year, he sent a very positive report about me to my superiors. Nonetheless, what I gained during those days of regency was marvelous. God truly inspired me to get into my natural talent of music by offering me necessary chances to develop that talent. Having had no training in formal music and having used the given chances only to vocal singing, I had no other experience in the music field. Fortunately, my parish priest, wrongly thinking that I knew how to play a church organ, asked me to play the music for the parish choir, which didn't have any organist. I was flabbergasted and explained to him my ignorance. But as a messenger sent by God, he encouraged me, saying, "You are a good singer, and you know the music usage. Why not you try to play? Learn it at your free time."

Actually, I had plenty of free time. So I practiced. The organ, which seemed to be a monster in the beginning, became my ancilla, and added to it, my sweet ancilla inspired me slowly to get into music-composing techniques. Again I say it was all a miracle. Without any formal training in such instrumental, vocal music, as well as in music composition, I began my ministry of music, only for the Lord and his church. I acknowledge with gratitude the contribution offered by my parish priest, without whose encouragement, I would not have been a musician as you see me today. In addition, besides developing a taste for priestly life by closely watching all the pastoral activities of that simple and holy country priest, I learned a lot from him on how I should be a dedicated servant of the Lord.

Dasan: So as you say, regency time was truly another milestone in your call to priesthood?

Ben: Absolutely. As I pointed out earlier, you paved the way for me making a right choice to accept the regency and amicably choose to test my vocation in fire. That helped me very positively, by the grace of God, to make my priestly vocation as my personal choice and not an imposed one by my elders.

From the day I entered into my theological studies, I became so empowered by the lectures of our professors and all other extra readings in theology, morality, and scriptures. While my spirit was willing to proceed with my journey to priesthood, my "naughty" brain never stopped worrying me with big and bigger questions and doubts on the church and her dogmas. Professors and spiritual directors remarkably helped me in solving my problems as best as they could. One among them not only smilingly responded to my questions but also prophetically shared some of his thoughts about my personal issues. He said, "Amalan! I appreciate your curiosity and interest in knowing more about God, the church, and the scriptures. Don't stop it. It must be continued till your death, because God by nature is a Living Being, a dynamic Person who always moves forward. He likes those who go beyond and search for the beyondness of oneself. Never be discouraged if you are not satisfied with the status quo. You are called to go beyond as our church is moving forward through her Second Vatican Council." He was telling me this in 1964! I am sincerely thankful to him.

His words struck me and stuck to my heart till this day. That spirit of going beyond pressed me harder when I was sent to a rural parish to do my first year of pastoral ministry. That might be one of the impulses that brought me to America as a missionary!

Dasan: Amalan! Tell me your own grateful experiences during your mission works in the archdiocese of Madurai, which is historically labeled as the French Mission of the Society of Jesus.

Ben: My missionary endeavors can be grouped under three chronological phases: from 1972 to 1978, from 1980 to 1994, and from 1994 to this day (July 7, 2015).

Let me disclose the tears of gratitude I shed during my first leg of missionary journey. Soon after my ordination and my final months of immediate preparation to become missionary in the archdiocese of Madurai, I was sent by my bishop to a rural parish (after the second bifurcation of the archdiocese, it is now within the jurisdiction of the diocese of Sivaganga). This parish, consisting of six mission stations with its central parish, was once considered a cursed area with no proper water and travel facilities. Therefore, many priests warned and frightened me telling that the parish had been used as punishment area where only rebellious or useless priests were sent. You know me well, after the bitter experience of regency, nothing seemed to me worst placement. And during my theological studies, I developed within me certain positive mind-set, which repeats a litany: "*Bloom where you are planted.*"

It worked out very well. The parish where I was sent had Catholics-majority low caste people, but very faithful, loving, simple but very emotional ones. God wanted me to use all my histrionic talents, which attracted all those rural population, who were either coolies or farmers. I began realizing I myself is a true missionary sent by God. Till this day I esteem that parish as my first love.

Since my music and drama was already well-known in the parishes of my diocese, Catholics, especially the rural areas, and the poor, liked me. That admiration of those people encouraged me to survive for two years in that so-called cursed parish. I was filled with the gratitude for them. Usually, any "first love" stays in our inner sanctuary with its indelible mark. My first parish experience of gratitude and enthusiasm is very vivid even today and never permits me not to doubt the genuine faith and love of the laypeople I have been meeting for the past forty-five years.

Dasan: While you were there, I heard from my Jesuit colleagues about your "fate" of being thrown into some interior territory of the archdiocese and thus not offering right chances to continue your music ministry. Already in many churches in Tamil Nadu and in Sri Lanka and Singapore and Malaysia, your devotional songs and mass hymns were prevalently used. They thought the Tamil Church might lose your music ability. But as you pointed out, you had been a nonstop runner and came out from the darkened valley alive and more energetic as the phoenix.

Ben: In addition, at the end of my services in my first-love parish, with the strong recommendation of some senior priests in the diocese, I was moved to one of the largest city parishes to serve the church in three ways: While I was assisting the parish priest in that parish I was given a responsibility to be some sort of prefect in the newly started diocesan apostolic school to help the students in their high school studies and in developing their personality according to the heart of Jesus and their innate talents, I too was permitted to develop my own music talent, especially the Indian music. To my amazement, the pastor in that parish was none other than the mentor who helped me in my regency! I was sincerely thanking God for such coincidence. I served there under him for five years, maybe a sort of another regency period!

Dasan: I was aware of the difficulties you underwent during those years and how you abruptly discontinued your music study due to the heavy burden of so many pastoral activities you had to undertake. Even during those years, you published the third volume of your music compositions, and you composed and published a wonderful phonographic disc of some of your songs, which are still sung, heard, and appreciated in public media.

Ben: During this period, one day you shared with me an astounding news that you would be sent soon overseas for your higher studies. I was so delighted to hear it.

Dasan: Being aware of my ability to capture the attention of the hearers when I was preaching in the churches and knowing the public adulation for my oratorical skills, my superiors thought that I would be the right person to form the young Jesuits in effective preaching. So they sent me to the USA for special studies in rhetoric so that I could teach later the young Jesuits in my own Jesuit province back in India. In the USA, I was, for four years, in two universities. From one, I took masters in rhetoric, and from another, I took masters in homiletics.

When I was doing homiletics in a non-Catholic university, I came into contact with many non-Catholic seminarians and professors, and that experience opened my eyes to see Christianity through non-Catholic sects. It was a blessing to me.

Ben: Indeed, it was a blessing not only to you but to me too. My heart was ceaselessly aching for going beyond my superior in the seminary prophesied. While you were in Chicago, I wrote you about my longing to spread the Word of God through my artistic talents more effectively and in a more modern way. You took the trouble of getting me a place in Loyola University of Chicago to take up my masters both in religious communication media and in rural theater communications. You also made sure I got a residence in a local parish where I would stay and perform pastoral ministries as well as pursue my studies. For this, I am indebted to you for the rest of my life. Surprisingly, my superiors in the diocese, by God's inspiration, extended their helping hand and sent me to the USA only for two years as sabbatical leave.

While I was continuing my studies in Chicago, I became enlightened in many ways, mainly to love the true freedom and to breathe fresh air of dignified individuality. I experienced the warmth and concern of American Catholics in Chicago with no discrimination. They based their relationship with me on two grounds: one, I was a Catholic priest; two, I came from the third world. One was religiosity, and the other was compassion. I felt so grateful to those American Catholics who loved me and poured their love and concern for me as their own son and friend.

After I completed my graduate studies, by the advice of some of my priest friends in Chicago, I desired to stay back some more months to make some research for my new communication projects. However, thanks to my guardian priest, in whose residence I was staying, I was exhorted with the yardstick of Catholic obedience (I hope you know, like you religious diocesan priests also make vow of obedience) to rush back to my diocese. Again my childlike faith and holy fear engulfed me, and that was how I reached my bishop's house and presented myself to my superior, saying loudly, "I am present, bishop."

Besides my faith and fear, my spirit was suggesting to me that I did the right thing. This is also a way to show my gratitude and respect to my guardian priest in Chicago for his generous hospitality and the same to my local bishop, who permitted me to pursue my higher studies in America.

I like to know from you what happened after you return from your higher studies and how you ended up being a missionary.

Grateful to the Calls within the Call

Dasan: Equipped with two masters, I returned home. Soon I was given a duty of educating young Jesuits. I am sure you remember I invited you once to Jesuit juniorate to compose some songs for a drama production. Our students were very happy and expressed their admiration to you. My ten years with them was a thrilling period for me, especially that they kept me young in mind, in spirit, and in body. As I was teaching young Jesuits rhetoric and public speech techniques, I used to visit various theological institutions to give courses on the same subjects. It was through me that in many seminaries and theologates in India, a new syllabus for homiletics started. Actually, I became so wearisome and tired of multiple works I had been committed to.

Ben: I still keep a vivid memory of two of us sitting alone in a restaurant and discussing about various happenings in our priestly ministries. I communicated to you about my undertakings after I returned from the States, full of freedom, dignity, and enthusiasm, of helping to "conscientize" rural and poor people in my diocese. While I was breathing fresh priestly air of independence and coexistence based on the golden rule of Jesus, I had many obstacles and rejections, which later I shared with you. You also disclosed to me your burdens in your works in the vineyard. You plainly described it this way: "Amalan, I am in the midst of a crisis. I feel honestly getting sick or even feeling dead psychologically. In this case, I am afraid I have become a more institutionalized than a charism-filled person." Not knowing what answer I should offer you, I simply suggested that you should take some sabbatical leave or a long retreat, which your society permits.

Dasan: Thanks, Amalan, for reminding me of that special discussion. During those hectic days, I prayed intensely but still continued to fulfill my commitments. I had been invited to teach homiletics in various Catholic institutions. It was in one such visit as guest professor in Bangalore I met a bishop from Malaysia. My gratitude goes to this bishop, who has been the primary cause of my missionary journey. The Malaysian bishop persuaded me to come to his diocese in Malaysia, and after writing repeated letters to my provincial, he got permission for me to go to Malaysia. Thanks to God, this is how I became an international priest, a true missionary of the global church.

Ben: Brother, I was so glad and thankful to God that he made you rise up and walk in his footsteps, carrying on the will of God to journey with him as Jesus did, wherever he let you. Share with me now your Malaysian experiences.

Dasan: Although borrowed garments never fit in well, I think I fitted well in the diocese of Melaka-Johor, and that is why I served there for a good period of unbroken seven years and borrowing me never led my Chinese bishop to his sorrowing. For the first two years, the bishop kept me in his own residence, which is also the diocesan pastoral center, where I saw lay Catholics from all the four ethnic groups of Malaysia working for the diocese. I realized that Malaysia is one of the few most peaceful countries in the world, although there live different races—Malays, Chinese, Indians, and Eurasians. Malaysians believe with Martin Luther King that "segregation on the basis of race is the adultery of an illicit intercourse between injustice and immortality."

Ben: You sent me many letters from Malaysia explaining like Paul how God made use of you for his kingdom's growth. While you were there, I was in the ministry of communications and media in the archdiocese of Madurai. Once I wrote to you requesting to arrange with your bishop to invite me and my artists to perform a two-hour multicultural programs in different parishes of Malaysia to educate and strengthen the faith of our Catholic communities. I was so grateful to you for your immediate response, for approaching your bishop, and he was ready to welcome our theater group. Your bishop consented to your request promising that he would meet all our travel expenses and provide us with a comfortable place to stay. Hearing this good news, you wrote to me about your admiration for the bishop for his generosity and broad-mindedness toward us, though we were artists who were Tamils and he was a Chinese. I tell you on that day I was overwhelmed in tears of gratitude for the biggest blessing I received from the Lord through you and your bishop, and so were all my artists.

Dasan: Undoubtedly, it was a great surprise to me too. When you and your group arrived, you began your cultural tour, and I myself accompanied you. Your performances were well appreciated by our people, and I was honored by them for the trouble I took in organizing your tour. As you were, I too was filled with tears of gratitude. That moment was encouraging me to accomplish more in my missionary services.

The world knows that Malaysia is a Muslim country; its government has been trying slowly and stealthily to Islamize its laws. Therefore, the church in Malaysia has almost a pathological preoccupation with survival. It is this situation that has aroused the lay faithful to come alive with fearsome enthusiasm and rally around the hierarchy. The church is forbidden to convert Muslims, but a lot of Chinese have given up Buddhism and have become Christians. Most of the Chinese faithful are new converts and like to call themselves born-again Christians.

Priests are fully aware that the common trouble with some born-again Christians is that they are even bigger pain the second time around. But I have to attest that if the church in Malaysia is alive and vibrant today, it is largely due to its born-again but fully committed laity who come forward to work hand in hand with the clergy, and where there are no priests, they practically run the parishes. Therefore, I was not surprised that in the diocesan pastoral center, among other ministries, I also conducted every month a one-day formation session for the laity. I must be thankful for this great opportunity given to me by God to closely and very spiritually relate myself with many dedicated lay Catholics.

During my two years' stay with my Malaysian bishop, I frequently conducted Bible sessions for lay Catholics on how to read, to study, to pray, and to live the Bible. This program was organized because, as the deer thirsts for running streams, so do the Malaysian Catholics literally thirst for the Word of God. I also wrote in those two years a series of ten booklets in English as texts for the Diocesan Bible Correspondence course.

Besides all the missionary works I enlisted above, I was also in charge of conducting monthly retreats for the priests; there were only thirty-three priests, and most of them very old. However, I loved those old priests. These old men not only believed everything I said in my retreat talks to the clergy, but also, I must gratefully acknowledge these retreats helped my own unbelief.

I must say here that the greatest problem about old age is that it may go on too long. These good old priests and few other middle-aged ones used to drive four to five hours in order to come for the priests' monthly retreat and spent nearly two days in listening to talks, in praying, in sharing, and in relaxing together. The main purpose of the monthly retreat was our spiritual renewal as priests, fitted and gifted by the Holy Spirit to be pastors. During our monthly retreats, we set aside plenty of time for personal prayer. During the personal prayer time before the exposed Blessed Sacrament, we used to switch off all lights except the tabernacle lamp, for churches are the best for prayer that have least light, for then we can see God only.

Toward the end of my first two years' stay in the residence of the bishop, I was given the role of priest secretary to the Conference of Bishops of Malaysia, a responsibility I held till I left that country. It was a conference of seven bishops, including three archbishops. Although the bishops appreciated how well I did my secretary work, personally, I did not like that job because I was not a local priest yet appointed probably because there was no one available and my secretary work itself consisted of just listening, taking notes, and preparing a report to be sent to Rome.

Therefore, although I respect and revere those bishops as chief pastors of the church, to whom all of us offer loving obedience in faith, I must confess that as secretary, I felt that I was unfit and appointed by the unwilling to do the unnecessary. But I must tell you that the experience I gained by being present at those conference meetings was unique and enriching. Prior to this appointment, during the course of my life, I had attended many other conferences that looked to me as gatherings of important people who singly could not do anything and together could not decide that something could be done either. Whereas, at the bishops' conference, I could really feel that the bishops were pastors who recognized their responsibility to one another's diocese and looked upon themselves as friendly partners in the supreme task of nourishing the spiritual life of the faithful. I am grateful for this encounter with the reality of our church.

After two years in the bishop's house, I was sent to the cathedral parish as its priest in charge. As pastor of that parish, I thought my chief duty was to preach and teach the Word of God, to heal and feed the faithful with the grace of God, and to form them into a praying, spirit-filled, witnessing, and sharing community. But the official title given to me was administrator.

Unity is symbolized not only in the cathedral church but also in any parish church. For example, in my cathedral parish, there were four hundred English-speaking, two hundred Chinese, forty Indian, and ten ethnic families.

I faced such a problem of anonymity in my cathedral parish. I said to myself that if I was not going to be part of the solution, I would be part of the problem. I proposed to the parish that a solution could be to organize basic Christian communities (BCCs) within the parish, where everyone belongs to the same parish visibly united with their pastor but trying to live out among themselves the communal life of the church, as far as possible, on the model of early Christian communities, praying and worshipping together, reflecting and renewing together, loving and sharing together, and thus experiencing the joy of being both a community and communion in Christ.

Even as a priest, I was, for many years, allergic to anything charismatic because of the mystery and misunderstanding associated with it. But I made a charismatic retreat under the well-known charismatic priest Father De Grandis. It was conducted in the pastoral center of my own Melaka-Johor Diocese. Four bishops and nearly one hundred priests from all over Malaysia made it with me. Thanks to the Almighty, after that retreat, I was drawn toward Charismatic Movement and became an active one of the regular ministries of our charismatic group in the parish, because when the Holy Spirit comes, he comes with healing in his wings.

Now I want to mention another renewal program, in which I was passionately engaged and one I conducted twenty times over. This is called parish renewal experience (PRE), originally started by an American Jesuit, Fr. Chuck Gallagher, which can serve also as a comprehensive and ongoing parish renewal plan. PRE is a weekend program, running for about twenty-two hours, spread out from Thursday to Sunday. It consists of eleven sessions with eleven presentations, which provide a basic adult catechesis on the key areas of Catholic life. Each session includes talk, prayer, scripture reflection, question and self-examination, and small groups and large groups sharing. On Saturday night, there is healing and reconciliation service called Shaloam Night. On Sunday, there is renewal of confirmation with anointing, and the whole program ends with a special Mass in which there is a ceremony of sending the participants on mission. This program strives to make the parish a living, loving, forgiving, and caring family of God's people. I am indebted to the Sanctifier in offering me a chance to join him in his sanctification work.

Ben: Brother, I am flabbergasted listening to your stories in your missionary life in Malaysia. As a brother and coworker in the Missions of the Lord, I thank the Lord for all your achievements for his glory and for his people.

Dasan: OK, Amalan. Here I have with me your bio data, which lists out all your qualifications to be effective and efficient missionary of the church. You have completed both a three-year diploma (BA) course in philosophy and a four-year diploma (MTh) course in theology at St. Paul's, Trichirappalli, India; you did receive two masters: one in pastoral studies in religious communications at Loyola University of Chicago, USA; the other in communication and theater arts at University of Illinois, Chicago, USA. What else did you do qualifying yourself to be fitted to perform missionary services in the USA?

Ben: God blessed me with energy and good spirit to undergo short courses in CPE, media ecology, Indian music, professionalism in communication, media education, power and play, and radio production. He too encouraged me to write and pass graduate English essay exam, TOEFL exam, and TWE exam. Besides, I underwent a two-year doctoral courses in ministry at Oral Roberts University, Tulsa, USA.

Unmistakably, I am grateful to the same Provider and the Sanctifier for inducing me to make the maximum and the best use of all my innate talents and acquired qualifications for his cause.

My response to God's call to serve as his minister in the church was nothing but living my whole life as a total offering to his cause. I might not have done so with my full heart and soul due to my human weakness. However, when I look back, the works I have carried out indicate that despite my failure to give full consent to his ways, I gratefully acknowledge he did grant me sufficient strength and wisdom to accomplish those functions that I enumerate here:

After my ordination for seven years, I worked as assistant pastor to two senior pastors. Serving in parishes as assistant or associate pastor may seem easier, but it needs certain amount of humility and tolerance to go in between the pastor and the people. Then for six months, I was promoted to be the pastor of a big rural parish, which was made of seven village churches. I too was asked by my bishop to serve as pastor in one of the newly created parish in a city. I served there for two years while I was building up a new communication center in the archdiocese.

Among those first seven years of my priestly life, I was given many responsibilities both in the local parish and the whole diocese, such as assistant director, St. Pius X Petit Seminary; coorganizer, Diocesan Bible Exhibition; director, Archdiocesan Youth Commission; organizer and director, Justin Rural Community

Theater; secretary, Archdiocesan Commission for Social Communication; organizer and director, St. Joseph Parish Community Theater; manager, Jai Christhu Publications; manager and correspondent, eight primary and secondary schools; chaplain, Central Prison; chaplain, Mother Theresa's Home for the Poor and the Forgotten; and organizer and conductor, Ecumenical Carol Services in the city.

Soon after my higher studies in the USA, I was summoned by my local archbishop to work on my communication projects relevant to and feasible for my archdiocese. Therefore, the diocese left me free from all pastoral commitments, and consequently, I was offered to undertake all possible efforts to build up a new center of communication. I was grateful to both my bishop and his diocesan managing team for such move. Unfortunately, my dream of establishing a center exclusively for communications didn't work out. After seven years of much heartbreaking and hard work, it was realized.

However, within those seven years, I never lost my hope and faith. As regular litany, my heart was singing within me, "Bloom where you are planted."

Being named as secretary and treasurer of the Archdiocesan Commission for Social and Cultural Activities, I formed a large theater troupe and christened it as Sathangai. It consisted of more than fifty performing artists—young and old, boys and girls. I took the troupe all over my diocese and even other dioceses in South India. Within my financial capacity,

I constructed a small recording studio at the building the bishop entrusted to me and published from there many audio cassettes of devotional and social songs. I put my heart and soul to these projects as pilot ones. They yielded their fruits. Both the local and the universal church became fully aware of my personal ability and dedication and started helping financially my new center to blossom. While the diocese offered me a new land in the outskirts of the city, the Vatican and mission and Caritas International agencies in Germany poured into my hands lavishly their funds. In 1988, the cardinal, Mother Theresa, the local bishops, and other dignitaries came to bless the new Sathangai Center, which included a main office, a professional and well-equipped recording studio, a multipurpose hall for trainings and workshops, boarding and lodging facilities for students attending courses conducted in the center, and a vast area with open-air theater facility. All these were possible only because of God's blessings and surely due to the loving cooperation of my well-wishers and the Christian and Hindu artists and volunteers. I am duly grateful to them.

Dasan: I know very well the stunning accomplishments you made during those years. I attended many of your open-air theater performances and thanks the Lord for his works wrought in you. I too was proud of myself and thanked God for this that he has used me as the initiator of all those amazing things.

Ben: I am indebted to you, brother, for everything you were to me. Whenever I get occasions, I am used to recognize your contribution in my life and ministry, not only in my personal mails and e-mails but also in my first publication, *SONDAY SONRISE*, and dedicating it to you, I wrote, "*My brother Fr. Vima Dasan SJ was my inspiration to become a priest. He has been, till this day, a role model to me in my spiritual and ministerial life through which he wants me to be fully fulfilled as he has been. Thanks to him, I am what I am today as an efficient religious communicator in the vineyard of the Lord. Being a prolific writer and effective homilist, he continues to be my critic, editor, and encourager as well.*" I am now interested to hear from you the encounters you faced with gratitude in England, the second leg of your missionary journey.

Dasan: Noticing that I was successful in building the parish into a community, the bishop thought that I would be also successful in demolishing the cathedral itself and in rebuilding it anew. So by his order, we pulled down the cathedral, raised $150,000, and rebuilt it; by the time the new cathedral was ready, I felt I myself was about to collapse physically, so I excused myself to the bishop, and on the kind order of the provincial, I left Malaysia and went back to the province. Within a year, I landed in England for further pastoral ventures.

Since my account of pastoral experiences in Malaysia has gone very long, I will state the bare minimum on my pastoral experiences in England. I arrived in the parish of New Market, of the diocese of East Anglia, in 1993. I was there for five years as assistant. I shared with the parish priest in the weekend and daily masses, also in conducting funerals, weddings, and baptisms. In the beginning, I used to make visits to the parishioners' families but found that the people were not interested in the clergy visits unless someone is sick at home or invited for some special occasions. But regularly, I took Holy Communion to the homebound.

A word about Mass attendance would be appropriate here. My parish had five thousand people in the register, scattered around six villages. In the main parish church, we had three masses on both Saturday and Sunday. Although about 450 to 500 people came for these masses, we had also two substations where we went every Sunday to say morning and evening masses. The attendance there would be about thirty. In general, church attendance in Britain was decreasing and likely to decrease faster in the next few years. The percentage of attendance by adults was 11 percent in 1980, 9 percent in 1990, 8 percent in 2000, and in 2005, it would be 7 percent. On any Sunday, 4 percent of those who sometimes attended would decide not to; 750 would leave each week because they no longer found church meaningful to them. There were 1,600 churchgoers who died every week; 750 would leave each week because they didn't like the minister or the people. The number of young people in the church was decreasing fast. Sixty-seven percent of the decrease in church attendance in the 1980s was of those under twenty, so was 55 percent of the decrease in the 1990s.

As an assistant, I had a lot of free time in hand. When I was wondering what to do with this time, the parish priest and parishioners asked me to publish my Sunday sermons in the parish newsletter. I took three days to write out one Sunday homily that was publishable. So it kept me busy. One of my parishioners, who was himself a publisher, made two separate collections of my sermons and published them in two books: *Wounded Deer Leaps Highest* and *Water on a Drowning Mouse*. In my fourth year in that parish, one of the Catholic weeklies in Britain, the *Catholic Times*, asked me to write for their paper a series of Advent and Lenten reflections, which I did. In the same year, a monthly magazine based in London called *Catholic Mission* came forward to publish a series of twelve articles written for people seeking some guidance from the Word of God for their troubles in life.

A few months before I left my first parish, St. Paul Publishing (London) expressed a wish to publish all my Sunday homilies for all three-year cycle, which I had preached in that parish. But they wanted me to write twenty more for special occasions, which I had not done. I agreed. So I took two weeks from my annual holidays, went to Rome, stayed in the Jesuit curia, wrote all twenty, and returned and sent them to St. Paul's, and this book, *His Word Lives*, was published in a few months after my arrival to my new parish. This book became a best seller in England and Ireland. It was published as an Indian edition by St. Paul's in India, where it has gone for second edition.

When my term of five years in the parish of New Market was nearing its end, I was packing to return to the province. But the bishop, by now a new one, requested the provincial to extend my stay in his diocese. It was extended, and I was sent to my present parish of St. Henry Walpole, in Burnham Market, as its parish priest. St. Henry Walpole was a Jesuit, born in a small village very near to my parish. You can see even today his baptismal entry in that parish register, but the place does not have a priest; I am their parish priest. St. Henry Walpole was executed with Edmund Campion during Reformation in the Tower of London.

My parish consists of a tiny community of Catholics, about sixty-four families scattered around about ten villages; most of them are above sixty. I have a daily Mass, attended by a handful. In winter, I have thirty-five to forty-five people in Sunday. As the weather improves, the attendance increases, so that in summer, the attendance would be from forty to sixty. The church can accommodate about eighty. On Easter and Christmas, the church will see an overflowing crowd. Many of them come over to this village to spend their summer holidays, which explains the increase in number of attendance during summer. Although it is a very small parish, the bishop thinks that if it does not have a resident priest, even this tiny community will gradually melt away both in faith and in number.

Besides my Catholic church in this little village, there are four more churches: two Anglican, one Methodist, and one Gospel Call. During Lent, we have weekly ecumenical services in each denominational church by turn. We have a few other ecumenical prayer services during the year. In fact, when the bishop sent me here, he told me very frankly that I will have a good amount of free time and advised me to write.

Faithfully following his advice, I began to write. I wrote 365 reflections for the millennium year, and St. Paul's (London) published it under the title

Daily Spiritual Reflections. Daughters of St. Paul in the Philippines have also published it in their country. I wrote daily reflections for Advent and Lent. Another Catholic publisher in Britain published them under two titles: *Advent Light* and *Lenten Light*. I wrote daily homilies for the two-year liturgical cycle, and St. Paul's (London) published them under the title *His Word for Today*. Daughters of St. Paul in the Philippines are also publishing it in their country. The Catholic Truth Society (CTS) brought out another of my small book, *Hope in Adversity*. In fact, I wrote it for myself, but they found it useful for many others.

Dasan: Originally the bishop asked the provincial to allow me to stay here for three years. But toward the end of this term, he got from the provincial an extension for another three years.

Ben: Let me say, in addition to what you have expounded, I heard from you within three months, St. Paul's (London) have asked you to write daily homilies for the seasons of Advent, Christmas, Lent, and Easter, which have become well-read in the globe. Let me list out those books as I found in my home library: *Wounded Deer Leaps Highest, Hope in Adversity, Advent Light, Lenten Light, Daily Spiritual Reflections, His Word Comforts, His Word Challenges, His Word Lives (ABC), His Word Is Life, His Word for Today, His Word Is Light (ABC), Preaching Sharp, and Love Retreat*. I hope I have sufficiently covered all your publications. And I heard from you that while you were still in London, every fortnight, you wrote three Sunday homilies needed for the *New Leader* (India), which you sent to the magazine by e-mail. We know very well that these homilies were not from your already published homilies. They were written keeping Indian context and readership in mind.

Dasan: Your list is okay. I am grateful to the Lord, as well as my society, which welcomed and approved of my missionary works in press media. Amalan! It was a big surprise to me when I heard from you that you had plans to go to the USA and, if needed, stay back in America. Even though you were accomplishing so many unimaginable services for the people in India as the sincere young missionary of God, explain to me, what brought you to make such decision?

Ben: When I returned from the States, I felt sorry to see the environment in the diocese was not as I expected it to be. The same rift and division among priests in the name of caste got worse and continue to demonstrate its unruly face against my sincere and dedicated Catholic communication ministries. Nonetheless, I tried to bloom where I was planted. As you mentioned, I did so much to the church and the non-Christians as the Spirit of the Lord moved me. I began working as the founder and executive director, Sathangai Academy of Arts, Culture, and Communication; I served as the principal of Sathangai Evening College of Performing Arts. Within the academy, I organized and conducted courses with my Sathangai Education Team such as seven one-month intensive courses in development communication techniques for social workers and social welfare officers from various parts of India, eighteen ten-day workshops in effective application of various development communication projects at the grassroots level for both voluntary and governmental officers and field workers from Block Development Department and Family Welfare Department, three two-week workshops in performing arts for religion and development for religious workers from all parts of India, twenty-two one-week workshops in social awareness theater projects for rural youth of Tamil Nadu, five six-day workshops in nonformal techniques in people's welfare education for social workers from all parts of India, thirty one-day sessions on innovative communication techniques for governmental field officers from Mother and Child Welfare Department, nine one-day sessions on media education for students at high school level, and sixty two-hour sessions on theater dynamics for city youths.

Dasan: Furthermore, I understand you also were engaged in communication enterprises out of the diocese. You served three years as secretary/treasurer, UNDA/OCIC/INDIA, an international Catholic organization for radio, television, and cinema (now it's named SIGNIS). For two years you worked as editor for *Catholic Sevai*, a diocesan monthly. You served as honorary probation officer at Central Prison, Madurai Region, and you also assisted the Diocesan Commission for Ecumenism as its secretary.

Ben: Yes, brother. Besides all the above responsibilities, I tried to compose and publish a number of devotional, social songs and carols. In the midst of all these, I never failed my Master Jesus in serving religiously and spiritually in local parish churches. Whenever chances arise, I conducted services at the altar and preached homilies that could elicit our congregations to the primary purpose of their lives; I too conducted many one-week retreats to nuns, college and high school students, and surely, for parishioners. I never missed chances of taking my theater troupe to many parishes in and out of the diocese; I produced and directed, if counted, twenty stage dramas, two sound-and-light performances, five dance dramas, and two multimedia shows and staged them in more than 250 places. I staged in more than twenty places my special multistage musical performance *Life of Mary in Pop Music*. The last but not the least, from the thesis I wrote for my masters in theater communication at Chicago, I invented the "EDU-CLOWNS," an innovative experimental street theater, designed as a social welfare educational project and implemented in two hundred places in Tamil villages.

After serving almost fourteen years at Sathangai Communications Center, as you felt many years back, I sensed I was at the low tides of my life. I was at the brink of collapsing both mentally and spiritually. My inner drive hushed in me, "It's enough. Get out for your holistic health." I longed to have a break. Due to my heavy program schedule, I didn't pay much heed to the inner voice. So God worked mysteriously as he did to me in the past. I was surrounded from all corners of the society by many ill-willed men and women who joined hands together and strangled me psychologically by their inhuman and unchristian dealings. I really felt the necessity of saying good-bye to all my histrionic performances and all public popular undertakings. While I was undergoing such crisis, you were already in London. You couldn't do anything about it.

Thanks to God, my local archbishop came to my rescue. He gave me three years as, we can say, sabbatical leave, and permitted me to pursue my doctoral studies in communications anywhere around the globe. My first preference was America for two reasons: the taste and smell of the American freedom and Christian love were evergreen in my heart and soul, and America still stands as the mother of inventions in the field of new media communications, and I also was familiar with its cultural situation that I can easily be immersed in.

Dasan: When you left for America, I think you esteemed it as a three-year sabbatical to pursue your doctoral studies in your favorite field of theater communications. Why then did you choose to stay back in the States to work as a missionary in Oklahoma?

Ben: It is a very long story, but I can summarize it here for you. First of all, I have to acknowledge the mysterious movement of God in humans' lives, and so it was in mine. With firm conviction to complete my studies, I landed in Brooklyn, New York, and got a parish to stay, to work, and to search for the opportunities to realize my dream. Unfortunately, I couldn't stay longer there because I was told it was only a summer assignment. After hard efforts, I got a very large parish in the same area and employed as associate pastor with other three more. Unfortunately, that placement was not conducive to pursue my studies because I was instructed that first thing first, I should work as a full-time associate. I found it hard to spend my hours in my studies, though New York University was ready to admit me to the initial courses for doctorate. Again I was seeking some other openings in surrounding dioceses but failed. I didn't lose my heart. I decided to finish my studies one way or the other within the three years bestowed by the bishop. I prayed hard and begged God to direct me. One day I discovered that Father Slattery, under whose guardianship and residence I had finished my masters in Chicago, has been elevated to bishopric. He moved to Tulsa, Oklahoma, as its bishop. When I contacted him immediately to my surprise, he warmly welcomed me to come and work in his diocese. But I told him about my plan of pursuing my studies. He encouraged me, saying that there were many universities there in Tulsa and that he would allow me to fulfill my ambition. That is how I ended up in Tulsa.

Dasan: While I was still in London, I heard from you this good news, especially of serving the Lord under the able hands of Bishop Slattery, with whom I too had acquaintance while I spent my days in Chicago. You too called me and said that you were appointed as pastor of two churches and that you were also permitted to pursue your doctoral studies in one of the Christian universities at Tulsa.

Ben: Yes, Dasan. I am grateful to God for prompting Bishop Slattery to show such benevolent gesture toward me. I didn't know at that time God had a different plan for me. He has been always a Surprise Giver to me as well as an efficient Potter and Plotter in my life's journey. After so many incidents that occurred in my life at that time—negative and positive as well—I was let by him to discontinue my pursuit of becoming a doctor in ministry, and he too ruthlessly separated me from my passion of histrionic arts and media. I say now, he truly cornered and fixed me to be more like a son, a missionary, of his heart. I was ironically made into a naked and simple country priest in the diocese of Tulsa. In addition to all these, I worked behind my bishops, both in India and in Tulsa, to position myself as a lifelong missionary of Oklahoma. Both bishops blessed me with offering me incardination in the diocese of Tulsa and with needed documents to become an American citizen. On one side, God became victorious in handling me the spoiled brat and his baby sheep; on the other side, he made me feel good about the realization that my heart's litany "blooms where I am planted." I was so glad that my aching to give back to America what I received from her was placated.

Dasan: Amalan! When you once wrote to me on your stopping all your music and other performing arts ministries, I was really unhappy; I too advised you to rethink about this. But when we later met in person, you shared with me about God's marvelous deeds behind all that had happened, I became convinced of the truth about your holdings. As I was looking back of your past years, I too started thanking God for all that he was accomplishing in both of us. Praise the Lord!

Ben: Let me close the description of my grateful tears shed in my missionary life in America with a few more testifying details of how God worked his plan through me.

I am a new immigrant to America, God's country and the land of dreams and opportunities. I also must be proud to say thankfully that I live and serve standing and walking on a holy ground where too many religious faiths are being melted and survive. The famous freedom consciousness respects all religions and faiths and yet keeps itself busy in search of the Ultimate. It is a fact only the body that finds itself fully content with all that it needs will allow the mind to go beyond itself and search for the Ultimate. As Osho, one of the Indian sages, pointed out, the "true search for spiritual things can be found only in an affluent society like America because it is not preoccupied with what to eat, what to wear, and where to stay." People who live in America have sufficient time to think of the spirituals; they have an inner drive to go beyond their boundaries. So we see so many young and old people in America who travel around, jump from one religion to the other, but always are in search of something beyond.

I was proud and grateful to be part of that searching crowd. I felt comfortable not only to be here but also in my Catholic priesthood because I was full here in my material needs. All my personal needs outside are well taken care of. I have enough time to be in search of the Beyond, the Ultimate. It is history that most of our theological findings and treatises came out of either the monasteries or the rectories. In both places, residents and inmates had enough food, shelter, and clothes. So they had ample time to go deeper for higher values and to dig into the mysteries that are beyond natural.

This is why America creates, invents, maintains, encourages, and even invites from other parts of the world so many evangelizers of different religions, different denominations, and different cults to preach about the Beyond, to talk about their vision and version of the Ultimate. Again I repeat that the reason for such attitude and behavior is not just its prosperity but also mainly its mental urge for the quest of the Ultimate.

America is God's country not only because it is blessed with prosperity and productive resources, not only because it has enough time and mind to search for the beyond, but also because it is blessed with abundant visions and dreams to go on mission to spread what they feel about the Ultimate, their own version of God, their theology about the world, life and the spiritual things. America also is so much blessed by God with effective and efficient tools for communicating the internal messages to other people far and wide. God very well blesses American communicators, especially those who communicate their version of the Ultimate, with the tactics of communication not just to inform people but also to persuade them for action.

I started my quest for the Ultimate while I was in the seminary where my material and physical needs were fully taken care of by the church. I never stopped searching till this day. I am grateful my quest and anxiety for the Ultimate doubled when I settled in America as a Catholic Christian missionary. More than ever before, I am now very intensively in search of the Ultimate. My personal testimony is that the American spirit feeds me, encourages me, and inspires me to go further and further in this quest.

In the midst of such searching journey, I am glad that I had been helping my fellow Americans who too try their best to know the Lord and much more to be like him. Together with my pastoral duties performed in different rural churches of Tulsa Diocese, I was very much concerned with their in-depth spiritual life. Besides, using my time in counseling, group discussion, and preaching and catechizing, I too, with the grace of God, wrote and published five books during the Year of Faith, 2012–2013.

Dasan: I am very proud of you, Amalan. I was very much surprised to see those five books you sent to me: *Sonday Sonrise, Daily Dose for Christian Survival, Prayerfully Yours, Catholic Christian Spirituality for New Age Dummies,* and *My Religion: Reel or Real?* More than yours, my eyes were heavy with downpour of tears of gratitude to our Lord, our parents, and surely, all our mentors.

The Tears of Joy

*Without joy, that person
is not a true believer.*

—Pope Francis

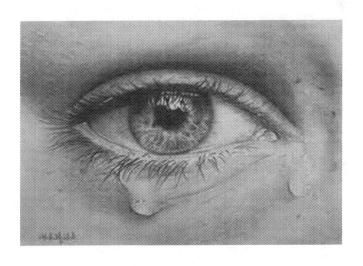

Ben: Writing about the tears of joy in human life, William Braud, California, wrote in one of his blog articles, *"Wonder-joy tears are not tears of pain, sadness, or sorrow. Rather, they are accompanied by feelings of wonder, joy, gratitude, awe, yearning, poignancy, intensity, love, and compassion. They are an opening up of the heart to the persons or profound circumstances being witnessed. These tears, with their accompanying chills and special feelings, seem to be the body's way of indicating a profound confrontation with the True, the Good, and the Beautiful—an indication of directly seeing with the eye of the heart, soul, and spirit."* Dasan! It is about this joy we both will share in this chapter. Though these can be interpreted as those drops falling down from our eyes due to the inner gratitude, the kind of tears we would be sharing here are those generated out of wonder and awe.

Dasan: I agree with you; it is like what the parents are feeling at the moments of witnessing their children's performances or any of their accomplishments. Becoming celibate priests doesn't mean losing our human parental sentiments. As any sensible persons would accept, all the products and fruits humans bring forth—be they children or discoveries that are spoken, written, sung, composed, and performed for other people's delight and life enhancement as well—are esteemed as babies produced from the human parental abilities.

Ben: As you pointed out, I recognize this fact of life throughout my entire life. As a true parent of my productions, which I bring forth in sweat and blood, I feel these wonder-joy tears are direct responses to the true, the good, and the beautiful. They are accompanied by positive affect—feelings of wonder, joy, gratitude, yearning, poignancy, awe, intensity, love, and compassion.

Dasan: With them also comes a feeling that our priestly heart is going out to what we are witnessing. The tears, chills, and special feelings come upon us, unexpectedly and spontaneously, as experiences of grace—as bodily signals, signs, or indicators of encounters with the numinous, as our body's way of letting us know we are having an unplanned, unavoidable encounter with the Real.

Ben: Here I have to confess that from the early days of my childhood, I was prone to be electrified by any creative and spontaneous products of others, especially my family members. I was used to love and choose only happy environments and make it a point to keep my personal situation always full of laughter and fun. This is actually something I learned from our family situation. Whenever all our family members join together in any place, the whole neighborhood would be bewildered to hear our loud laughter and talk. That is our birthright, and though our dad was so rigid in religious and moral matters, he was the best and funniest person in our crowd to keep every one of us feel free and funny. Unfortunately, when I entered seminary life, all those typical qualities of our family trait I possessed were curtailed in the name of discipline. Is that the way we the priests should consider our life—as frown and grim? Is it not true our Master Jesus, who called us to follow him, longs to see us joyful?

Dasan: Undoubtedly, that is the eternal desire of Jesus. That is why before he left us at his Last Supper, he underlined joy as our ultimate goal of priestly life. But we should be very clear about the meaning of the joy he referred to. We follow not an ordinary Man of Nazareth, but he is the truth, the life, and the resurrection. He definitively declared that he came to give us joy to the full.

Ben: You said it correctly, brother. Whatever you told me echoes what Pope Francis underscored elaborately in his homily at Holy Thursday's Chrism Mass, April 17, 2015. At the end of his preaching on the priestly joy, he prayed for all the priests this way: *"I ask the Lord Jesus to preserve the joy sparkling in the eyes of the recently ordained who go forth to devour the world, to spend themselves fully in the midst of God's faithful people, rejoicing as they prepare their first homily, their first Mass, their first Baptism, their first confession . . . It is the joy of being able to share with wonder, and for the first time as God's anointed, the treasure of the Gospel and to feel the faithful people anointing you again and in yet another way: by their requests, by bowing their heads for your blessing, by taking your hands, by bringing you their children, by pleading for their sick . . . Preserve, Lord, in your young priests the joy of going forth, of doing everything as if for the first time, the joy of spending their lives fully for you."*

Dasan: Yes, Amalan. In one of his daily masses, the pope is quoted saying that *"the joy of faith, the joy of the Gospel is the touchstone of a person's faith. Without joy, that person is not a true believer."* Explaining more about the Christian joy, he defined it as the joy of the promise, the joy of hope, and the joy of the covenant. That is the way I had been considering my inner joy and trying to keep it complete:

When I tried to be joined to Christ like the branch to the tree because he said, "*I am the vine, and you are the branches.*"

When I served my neighbors out of love for them and not out of selfish motives.

When I served the poorest of the poor, because he said: "*If you give a cup of water to the poorest, you give it to me.*"

When I joined with other Christians in ministry instead of doing it alone by myself. That is why Jesus had twelve apostles round him.

When I preached the Word of God to the faithful at Eucharistic celebrations.

When I preached the Word of God at retreats to the religious who have vowed to follow Christ in a radical way.

When I distributed Holy Communion to the faithful at Mass.

When I heard confessions and forgave sins and gave counseling to the penitents.

When I joined parishioners at Eucharist adoration and procession, which is a public demonstration of my faith in the Eucharistic Lord.

When I baptized babies and, especially, elders, remembering Christ's Qord: "*Go and preach to the ends of the world, and baptize them in the name of the Father, Son, and Holy Spirit.*"

It was these words of Christ that inspired me to travel to various countries as a missionary priest. Among the ministries that I enjoyed most has been preaching and, particularly, writing, for what I write remains for many years, unlike preaching. A source of joy to any priest is the development of his natural talents. I developed my speaking and writing talents early in my formation that always kept me fulfilled. And when these talents came to fruition, it gave me immense joy.

Ben: Likewise, you were joyful, I knew, when you heard and witnessed me developing my musical talents very early in my seminary days, which kept me longing for public performances, which won acclaim of all.

Dasan: Yeah. Still another source of joy for the priests in ministry is the appreciation and admiration we receive from people to whom we go to serve.

Ben: You said it right. In the beginning stage of my ministry as missionary for Christ, I very much liked it when the public were clapping their hands and getting close to me, requesting me to shake hands with them or even hugging me, as it is common in America. The worst thing I encountered in my entire occupation was the human popularity and patting on my shoulder and making me forgetful of the divine joy for which I was called for.

Dasan: Whatever joy we priests receive from the people is nothing compared to the joy we receive from Jesus Christ, who calls us to priesthood; he bestows us talents needed for our ministries and opportunities to serve the public behind whom he is always present.

Ben: Actually, in this chapter, we would be talking about our joy in our missionary life, which Pope Francis calls *"the missionary joy."* He says, *"It is the priestly joy which is deeply bound up with God's holy and faithful people, for it is an eminently missionary joy. Our anointing is meant for anointing God's holy and faithful people: for baptizing and confirming them, healing and sanctifying them, blessing, comforting and evangelizing them."*

Tears of Joy during Formation Years

Dasan: Let me first describe the joy I encountered in my formation time. Soon after I joined the Jesuit novitiate, as everyone felt, I too had some starting troubles, but I don't know how it came to be; my heart began beating a rhythm of joy. Later I realized it was surely the work of God's Spirit.

After I took my first vows, on the way when I was going to a parish on a hill town, I was struck with cholera. I was practically dying. I still remember vividly how some nuns stood around me holding my body, for I was in convulsions. But I did not die. Slowly the attack of cholera began to lose its grip on me, and soon I began to feel better. When I went home and was convalescing, my sister was attending on me day and night. When I completely recovered, I could not put into words the enormous joy I felt.

During my formation years in the society, every time I met my spiritual father for counseling, I experienced inner liberation and strength that generated within me certain unthinkable solace and joy. Every year I moved to one step higher in my educational field, especially when I won medals and prizes in the college for my studies in Tamil language, my joy was overwhelming. As a highlight of all the days, the day I was permitted to be ordained priest, my heart was genuinely singing, *"I've got the joy, joy, joy, joy . . . Down in my heart . . . Down in my heart—Where . . . Down in my heart . . . I've got the joy, joy, joy, joy . . . Down in my heart . . . Down in my heart to stay."*

Ben: I still remember my visit as a young village boy to your novitiate with our parents. Besides the sumptuous meals I enjoyed from the Jesuit hospitality, I was bewildered to notice your changed behavior—silent, walking with discipline, smiling but always keeping a distance as water under the lotus flower. Our parents too felt the same.

Dasan: I know. As you shared earlier, your formation years were somewhat turbulent ones. Were you totally in depressive mood all the time?

Ben: No, brother, no. Despite the horrific turmoil I had been downcast with, the famous lifesaving litany "Bloom where you are planted" was uninterruptedly ringing in my inner soul. I am sure it was 100 percent the Lord's deed. I had never been depressed in my formation years as I felt many years during my priestly ministry. Even if I was pushed downhill by the superiors' remarks or my own companions' in the seminary, I never stayed down for days; rather, within a few hours or a minimum of one day, I rose up and acted normal. There was some sort of happiness that boosted me—my laughter became louder, my singing took its highest pitch of tenor, and my conversation with my companions turned out to be hilarious and jovial. I knew, in later years, these things were not coming out of the true joy; rather, they were all happy moments I created as counteracting all my negative feelings—only reactionary deeds. Sometimes I did feel true joy in my heart during those years, such as whenever the congregations, who were spellbound and bemused by my histrionic ministries in their churches or public functions, appreciated and even contributed some monetary help for my personal expenses. It was again, I later recognized, the marvelous play of our God to preserve me intact for his purpose.

Dasan: When I explained the meaning of true joy of a priest, I didn't exclude the happiness we priests experience through our achievements and from our beneficiaries' satisfaction. You did all your cultural activities only as the priests of God do; you wore all the time, even on performing stages, your priestly garb with its red sash, which is a public symbol of witnessing our Master and boldly proclaiming to the crowd that you did everything for him and with him.

When my superiors offered me a chance to go to America for my higher studies, I was thrilled with tears of joy. That exhilarated joy continued to increase from the moment I stepped into the aircraft. It was because I got into the airplane for the first time in my life, heading toward the USA and seeing for the first time the famous New York City by night as the plane glided down, and I felt I was entering into a new celestial heaven. My joy became doubled when, at the airport, I saw and met my Jesuit friends who had come to escort me to their residence for resting.

Ben: Naturally as men born and bred in a village environment in India, where even the ground transportation and traveling facilities were very rare, both of us felt the wonder-filled joy at each one of us offered the chance to fly overseas. You too shared with me all the joyful experiences you had while you were in America. You wrote about your excitement when you once joined a group of American schoolchildren for boat travel along a beautiful river rounding its path around the forest and about the enjoyment you felt as you saw Niagara Falls thundering down its waters.

Dasan: I have to enumerate some more occasions when I encountered such elated joy: when an American Catholic family adopted me as one of their children and invited me to come for daily meal with them; at the end of my university studies when I obtained masters in communication and another masters, in homiletics, as I attended convocation. It was, indeed, a thrilling sight. This God-bestowed joy became more complete when he let me obtain admission for you in Loyola University of Chicago for your studies.

Ben: I fully understand all those moments of joy you had gone through during your formation period both in India and America. Let me tell you a bit of my joyful encounters during my stay at Chicago.

As soon as I entered Chicago, the first thing that gave me a big surprise was, thanks to you and Father Slattery, the entire environment bestowed to me my board and lodging, sufficient time to complete two masters within two years, all-embracing concern and love showered on me by local Catholics, and the inconceivable support and assistance granted to me by my university professors in passing my studies with flying colors though American English, I would say, was my third language, which I became acquainted with mostly within the first six months at Chicago. The joy and excitement dominated me so powerfully that I never cared for the inconveniences of a 10×10 room allotted for my stay in the rectory; I never worried about the hardships I underwent in traveling to universities either by walk or by public transportation, and I began creating a big taste for any food prepared in American style. The joy was astonishingly overwhelming! Let us now talk about our feelings of joy in our ministries.

The **Joy that Comes from Ministries**

Dasan: After I returned to my mother province, I was posted to Jesuit juniorate, and I was there for ten years. The joy that I inherited from the day of the last vows and ordination continued whenever I performed my priestly duties: While I was teaching in the juniorate, I had joy full to the brim because of the fact that I was forming many Jesuits of my province to become effective media persons, especially preachers of the Gospel. During those years as practical learning, I enjoyed taking every year Jesuit juniors on cultural tour to Chennai, the state capital as well as one of largest media centers in India; another dimension of my joy was my juniors stage dramas under my direction and winning acclaim from one and all.

Amalan! When you returned from Chicago with the two masters degrees and plunged yourself immediately into fulfilling your vision of new communication ministry in your diocese, I, as a helper in your life's development in some ways, felt immense joy as a sort of parental sentiment. Share with me more of your personal experiences of joy in those years.

Ben: From the studies I underwent in American universities, I decided to dedicate myself to empower our Indian rural people to help themselves in their development. For this, I considered arts and media as the effective instruments, not only because they are my innate and qualified professional skills but mainly because of the spirit I acquired from American educational researches that the famous American developmental elder underscored in his pithy quotations. He had said already on June 25, 1933, "*You must never tell a thing, you must illustrate it. We learn through the eye and not through the noggin.*" (Thanks to *Tulsa World Newspaper*, 7-18-15.) That was the primary reason for my obsession with visual, dramatic, musical dancing, and performing arts.

In regard to my joyful missionary activities: I love to divide that period in two phases: first seven years— from 1980 to 1987—while I had struggled very much for establishing myself and my vision among the church leaders and the priests in my diocese, my heart was trounced with joy because the people of Madurai and of Tamil Nadu appreciated and admired my earnestness; mostly non-Christians and non-Catholics became close friends and fans to me, and the local print media covered page after page their positive views about my cultural undertakings. Besides all these, many laypeople from all sections of Madurai City came forward to help me in my initial endeavors with either minimum or no remuneration whatsoever because they knew well financially I was in a desperate situation.

This joyful disposition impelled me to behave among my lay friends and, especially, my coartists, always as messenger of Jesus with sincere love and devotion to all my cultural missions; I worked with them night and day, gratifying them more by my love and respect and admiration rather than sufficient monetary rewards. In a way, I esteemed them—though they were of different religions, as comissionaries sent by Jesus in my missionary communications.

Dasan: I have witnessed all that you have enumerated whenever I had a chance to visit you. I was staggered to notice how those of your coartists worked with you day in and day out. I wished and prayed earnestly during those years that God would bless you, realizing your ambitious goal of building up a new communication center in the archdiocese. Explain to me, how did you finally succeed in realizing your awesome dream?

Ben: That is the story of one more milestone in my encounter with missionary joy. During this phase, God sent us two new archbishops who, in their own charism and wisdom, not only encouraged me and offered full freedom to pursue my dreams, but also they contributed their counseling on how to go about in their realization and helped and blessed me in getting support from the Vatican for the projects I submitted through them. Astonishingly, the Vatican and some other European Catholic agencies lavished thousands of dollars to implement almost all the projects I submitted to them. The whole of Tamil Nadu was astounded to notice the instant growth of the new center I constructed. It was totally my brainchild, which I birthed in agony but a sweet one, and I maintained it for nearly seven years as its founder and director. I enjoyed every bit of my contribution toward such phenomenal enterprise accomplished in sweat and blood. When one media interviewer asked me, "How is it possible for you to perform all your duties as jack-of-all-trades, acting as director as well as a guardian and promoter of this monumental venture?" I told him, "I do everything not just as a duty but as fun and game. I won't do anything, even its bit, if my heart is not enjoying." This response itself is a great testimony to the tears of joy I shed during those years when the hectic ministry full of rejections, doubts, betrayals, and misconceptions encircled me.

Dasan: You have to forgive me to add a bitter point to what you have enumerated. Many people who watched your untiring works during those years—especially many priests, nuns, and even our relatives and friends, including myself—sometimes suspected the worth of all those activities, and we disliked the way you dealt with your media communication ministries. Did you regret it?

Ben: Thanks, brother, for reminding me of this dark aspect of my ministries done as the director of Sathangai Communication Center. Yes, I was 24-7 cowed to my undertakings, forgetting all my relatives and friends; yes, I was always surrounded by young and old performers, singers, musicians, dancers, lyricists, playwrights and stage designers, and other media technicians. Though I was wearisome and tired, I had to put on a smiling face and to laugh, joking in their midst for the reason of making our hard works light and easy. Every time I brought out any stage or media productions, I was undergoing the pangs of birth, but as the scriptures verify, I felt joyful in my heart that I brought forth an artistic production of my own. Yes, I ignored relating myself to relatives and friends for the main reason I wanted to win over the hurt feelings I experienced when I, as an innocent and very naive lamb, was taken to the petit seminary and thrown out of the beautiful family environment that I had been cherishing as my haven. At one time, I think it was in my major seminary days, I began ignoring and leaving from that cherished memories of family and its ties, quoting to myself Jesus's strong words to his disciples: "*If any one comes to me without hating his father and mother, wife and children, brothers and sisters, and even his own life, he cannot be my disciple*" (Lk. 14:26). In one way, those words served as my purpose, but later I came to understand it was too utopian an interpretation of Jesus's words. Our dad too, whenever I met him in my formation period, repeatedly instructed me to be true to Jesus, quoting his discipleship demands. Yes, I was very much concerned about winning popularity and a good name among my crowds and fans. I tried my best to maintain that during those years. But unfortunately, it didn't work out well. The more I attend to my celebrity maintenance, the worse I encountered, which I will describe in the next chapter. Please share with me the joy you felt in your missionary endeavors both in Malaysia and Britain.

Dasan: I discussed with you already in the previous chapter about my activities in those two foreign countries, for which I am obligated to God and beloved humans in my missionary achievements. All those accomplishments truly offered me amazing joy, especially at those times when I baptized babies, when I offered masses and distributed the Eucharist to the sick and homebound, when I counseled spiritually so many parishioners thwarted by despair and depression, when I preached well-prepared and professionally delivered homilies, and when I continued to write regularly articles in church weekly bulletins and published books in English, mostly expounding the Word of God related to the modern needs of our Catholics, whom I was sent to serve.

I uphold up to this day the pleasant memories of so many Catholic laymen and laywomen, supporting me and encouraging me as angels sent by God during those years of foreign milieus.

Ben: Let me now illustrate the tears of joy I was filled with during my missionary works in America. After many attempts to find the right place to realize my "go beyond" dreams in that country, I was finally given the surprise blessings of the Almighty. When I heard from Bishop Slattery that I was accepted to join the diocese of Oklahoma, I was overjoyed for these main reasons: I got a safer place in a foreign country, especially under the bishopric of my longtime friend Bishop Slattery. Secondly, I was permitted to pursue my ambitious studies. Thirdly, as any adult would do, I esteemed it my pride to join with the other Tulsan priests in serving our Catholic communities as the first missionary from a foreign land with a different skin color.

As I started my pastoral works in the Tulsan Diocese, I was truly attracted by the simple but strong faith of Easter Oklahoman Catholics. Tulsan region has been ever recognized as a community that is one of the most generous communities in the USA. I saw it, I felt it, and I touched and certainly tasted its goodness and sweetness. With its cultural and historical background, the state of Oklahoma possesses tremendous inner drive to rise up and shoot out all possible distant stars—I mean, so ambitious and energetic to climb up the ladder of achievement. I was so enthralled to become one of those kinds of persons. As you know from my first year of priestly life, my life's motto is "Go beyond." The central focus of Oklahoman engagements is nothing but making a difference in life.

Dasan: I was glad that you got an appropriate diocese where you would pursue your studies. But my big surprise was the decision you made to stay back permanently. May I know why you didn't complete your doctorate and what made you become a full-time and lifetime missionary in America?

Ben: It is not only you who asked me that; there were many friends, both in America and in India as well, who were shocked by my choice. Let me explain myself here. In the first year in Tulsa, within three months of serving as associate in a very big city parish, Bishop Slattery, due to lack of priests for filling vacant parishes, and because of my seniority in priestly ministry, promoted me as pastor of a rural parish and its mission. That was a big turning point in my life for the fact my one and only ambition of completing my doctorate was slowly fading as I was fully obligated to serve wonderful Oklahoman Catholics within my abilities. Actually, it was their kindheartedness, their friendship, and much more their spiritual hunger that crisscrossed my dreams. Gradually, I understood my strength of being a full-fledged pastor serving my parishioners, fulfilling their needs and demands. Unfortunately, I couldn't finish my entire doctoral studies that should end with an applied project.

At this moment, my three years' sabbatical came to an end, so the Madurai bishop contacted me, inquiring about my return. He was, indeed, a godsent man who acted out in the place of my Creator.

He, in a friendly way, asked me, "Are you happy there, Amalan?"

I immediately responded, "Yes."

Then he surprisingly told me, "You must be happy wherever you are. That is my wish. If you find happiness there, continue to work there."

That was the starting point I consider now as God's definite clarion call for my missionary works in America. However, my inner longing to get doctorate in ministry at Oral Robert University, Tulsa, inducing me to pick up my final thesis work. Bishop Slattery, a good-hearted and understanding friend, yielded to my request, though he didn't like it. I was offered freedom to move from the pastoral works to Houston. I was happy I got admission in a Methodist hospital as CPE student. Actually, I was in the mood for becoming a freelance global preacher and communicator of Christ. Again God intervened in my life's gambling to go beyond. His design for me was totally different from mine. In addition to it, I knew within me certain nonstop restlessness despite the petty and transient happiness I experienced through my several moves to counteract my odds. Within three months, the Almighty arranged a critical event that put all my ambitions topsy-turvy.

Dasan: You shared this with me when I paid a visit to you when you came back from Houston. That was, I am sure, a thrilling experience of knowing how God can do marvelous deeds in us according to his design. Describe it to me again.

Ben: After a month when I joined the CPE summer course in Houston Hospital, one day I lost my billfold that contained all my ID cards and some dollars. It was so much needed for my life as I started my new life in a totally new environment of profession. I searched and searched it for two days. I couldn't find it. Finally, I knelt before God one morning in despair and grief. It was a Sunday. I did pray every day. But this time it was different. I proposed to God this way. I made a deal with him. "God," I said, "if you get that billfold and hand it over to me today and it should happen now as I am praying, then I promise I let you do in whatever way what you want me to do. If you prefer me going back again to Tulsa Diocese and be a sincere, simple, and committed pastor in a rural parish, as my bishop feels right, I will certainly obey you."

Amazingly, you will never believe this, as soon as I prayed this way, I heard my phone ringing. I answered the phone. Guess who spoke what? On the other end, one of my friends from the hospital said, "Hey, Vima, good news. You got your billfold. I give you the phone number. Just contact this man. He will tell you all details about this. I think you lost it some place in the downtown area." It took many hours for me to come out of the shock and thrill. I rushed to the home referred by my hospital friend; he handed me my billfold intact. I thanked him again and again. He too shared with me how he got the billfold. When he was going for a morning stroll with his dog, he got the billfold. What is a more astonishing factor in this incident is that first, the one who found out my billfold was his dog, which got it and gave it to his master, and second, his master was a Baptist deacon who encouraged me to come and join his church group to take away my isolation! That is how God cornered me repeatedly as a wise and powerful person but always a kind and compassionate Father.

As I was thankful to God for obliging my request, I confirmed to him in prayer that I would leave back to the diocese as soon as my summer course was over. On the same day, I contacted Bishop Slattery. Very interestingly, he, who is very busy, especially on Sundays, took the phone immediately. I told him of my desire to come back to serve in the diocese.

Unbelievably, he replied, "Vima, I knew well you would contact me. You have been always with people. You would not survive in that lonely and isolated environment." Then he added, "Come soon after your course ends. I have a place waiting for you."

What a profound game God was playing with me! His ways are high ways. If he decides to pin down his chosen ones to his designed mission, he will spare no time. You can see how quickly the series of his actions happened one after another! I heard him repeatedly in my inner sanctuary: "Go beyond, my son, from your fake self and vain glory. Behave like my Son Jesus, your elder Brother! Leave everything, I mean everything, even your very ambitious self."

When I replied, "Like your Son, here am I Lord. I come to do your will," a perfected joy was filling my soul. Please permit me to say one more thing regarding the concept of priestly joy. When Jesus promises that our joy would be complete, I don't think he was referring to the completeness of our joy that will never happen until we reach his mansions; rather, what he meant was that our feeling of joy would be by and by, gradually perfected as we act according to his will fully and holistically. Is that correct?

Dasan: Of course! While you were working in Tulsa Diocese, I know how friendly your bishop was. He had permitted you to incardinate yourself to his diocese with the full blessing of your Madurai archbishop; he granted all the helps you needed to become naturalized as an American citizen. When I visited Bishop Slattery, he explained to me how parishioners loved you and accepted you, though you were foreigner, as their friends. I was, indeed, so happy about this news and even tempted to join you to work in your diocese, but it was God's will again, and I was not permitted by my superiors. That way my personal joy became more perfected. Now, Amalan! Tell me how your parishioners increased your missionary joy in Oklahoma?

Ben: Sure. I have served for twenty years in nine churches as the global church's missionary in Tulsa Diocese, OK. Except the six-month service at a city parish as an associate, all the other churches were rural. I was filled with priestly joy when I served those Oklahoman Catholics for a number of reasons: First, there was something unique about my parishioners— both cradle and new converts as well—that roused joy in me. Their qualities were combined in such a way that they were in a class by themselves—unusual, extraordinary, and unforgettable. Most of the men were gentlemen, and the women were ladylike, in the classic sense of the terms. They would never knowingly inflict pain on another; they avoided the clashing of opinion or suspicion or gloom or resentment; they were tender toward the bashful, gentle toward the distant, and merciful toward the absurd. Many of them were of few words, never spoke of themselves except when compelled, had no ears for slander, never insinuated evil, and had too much good sense to be affronted by insults.

Secondly, those parishioners whom I had assisted while they ailed and helped them at their final hours with rituals and compassionate presence were all, I would dare enough to call them, the real champions, or knights, of Christ, because every one of them submitted to pain because it was inevitable, to bereavement because it was irreparable, and to death because it was their destiny. Thirdly, I have encountered almost in all of them certain magnanimity that never let their sufferings and hardships make their spouses, children, and relatives be disturbed. The awesome element that filled joy in me was noticing almost all of them have been blessed with natural gifts from God at their birth, such as high IQ, inheritance, family prosperity, racial background of hardworking ability, physical stamina, and so on. They made the best use of all his natural resources and blessings in the right time, right place, and for proper results. Very many men served their country honorably in the United States Army during the many wars around globe; when they came back to their neighborhood, they continued their chivalrous undertakings, which were good for both their families and the communities. Before they got married, both men and women mutually searched and dated seriously to choose right life partners. While men among most of the senior parishioners sought out a job, even if it was a hard, laborious one but which could bring about sufficient money to take care of their family members, women, on their part, were working day in and day out as homemakers, rearing up their children, educating them in secular and religious matters. As common in all parts of the world, while men were so busy and distracted in their earnings and prosperity and safety and security of their homes, women were the ones who brought their children and stepchildren to the church, admitted them in parish catechism school, and witnessed their Catholic faith by their piety and faith-filled prayer and devotion to the saints.

One of the most admirable behavior of these men and women that put me spellbound was their strong willpower combined with faith throughout their hard journey of life. Let me give an example: One of my beloved parishioners was George, who always loved his church and never missed Sunday and Holy Day services until he became weak and fragile due to his ailment. I never heard him bragging about himself; he never blew the trumpet of his achievements. He possessed an unassuming personality and never intervened in any politics of the parish. He never made any complaint about his sickness. When he got sick and had difficulty walking, I approached him and inquired about his health whenever he attended Mass accompanied by his wife. He always smiled at me, held my hands firmly, and used to say a few words: "I am okay, Father. Please pray for me," showing his hands and legs that gave him terrific pains. That means he wanted me not only pray later but also requested me to offer him a healing touch of the Holy Spirit. I gave it more often lovingly and sincerely. That was how he died restfully and painlessly. His wife later testified to me that just a few seconds before he died, she saw his face getting brighter, smiling, and looking at her, and she heard him mumble, "I made it." Even though it was a big blow to me, as I considered him as my close friend, it was a sweet agony to hear his wife's testimony.

Another joyful experience in my missionary works was having so many lay volunteers, especially women, who cooperated with me in my pastoral activities. Above everything else, I found joy as Jesus had whenever he visited Bethany, the home of Mary and Martha, who would host him with tender, loving care. It is not just at the times they invited me to their homes for meals but also at the times when they were in the parish hall of every church that I could feel my joy overflowing as I witnessed these Catholic women, both young ones and seniors, like Martha to Jesus, cooking, preparing tables, and serving sumptuous food to me and the entire parish family. If I missed any one of it, that was the end to me. One after another would contact me and inquire about my absence, or some of them would reserve a special food package for me to eat later and would bring it to me when I was at home. These were all God's deeds for me to reconcile with my negative thoughts of the past, telling me that instead of having one physical mother and dad, he has been offering me so many mothers and fathers and sisters and brothers who took good care of me.

In my administration, sometimes when I became so depressed and expressed it in the finance or parish councils or mostly in my private conversations with a few parish well-wishers, some would never say anything, just smile. Those smiling faces encouraged me so much that when I was closely related to those persons, emulating their willpower, I convinced myself to prove my worth too and started changing my negative approach to positive. Thus, I can say I had accomplished many things more than I could achieve in those churches. Diplomacy was not at all my strength;

rather, my loving, transparent, honest and dialogical and communal approaches saved me, as those qualities drew many supporters and helpers from my congregations.

The last but not the least of my joyful experience was noticing the enormous generosity of my parishioners. As wonderful stewards of the Lord, whenever I invited them to perform some laborious and time-consuming jobs in and around the church buildings, they volunteered with no hesitation, but they made sure from me whether that work was worth doing. As in every Catholic parishes in the Western world, the parishes I served also consisted of a majority of seniors who lived either by their pension or their social security check. What made me bewildered was, these seniors were the sole contributors to the church who put their gifts in regular and extraordinary collections. Most of these seniors regularly attended Eucharistic celebrations.

In one of my parish bulletins, I wrote about these seniors in a spirit of appreciation and rejoicing: "*You are bold and honest enough to claim, 'I am the church, I make the church, and therefore, I run the church.' Such daring claim is possible only for you who sincerely hold on to the wonderful, mystical Eucharist connections with the Lord and other members of your local church.*" I was edified seeing their generous and untiring stewardship spirit and showing it outside with no reservation. Faith-filled life, committed stewardship, humble generosity, and high-spirited Catholicism are, I can underscore, some of the synonyms for defining the parishes I served in the diocese of Tulsa. My only duty as pastor was to encourage and develop in my parishioners such Catholic Christian spirit.

Dasan: Amalan, God never let you down; rather, he preserved you, as the Bible says, under his wings. He was, in many ways, taking you through living waters and green pastures. One more thing I should mention here about your ministry of writing, which made both of us filled with joy, was that when I was working as missionary in England in one of your trips to India from Oklahoma, I met you at Heathrow Airport for a while. Just then my first monumental book, *His Word Lives*, was released through St. Paul's Publication in London. I took a copy of it with me to the airport to show it to you.

Seeing that book, you said, "Brother, I will one day publish a similar book."

I am very proud of you that you kept your word, and to this day, you have published six books in English, all on the Word of God, religion, and spirituality. You have been sending me a copy of it. Going through those books, I have been immensely elated. You too, I am sure, were joyful in reconciliation with God who, you thought, had hurt you by not blessing you completely with your doctorate. I would say sincerely your books are more than doctoral theses, especially the books on Catholic spirituality and on prayer life. Whenever I think of your past and my connections to those years in your life, I feel happy overwhelmingly and thank God that I have been your mentor and inspiration not only to your vocation to missionary life but also to your writing apostolate.

Ben: During my active missionary life in America, God directed me to help and support the needy in South

India, where I was born and bred and grown and formed to be his priest. In this way, he designed that my inner spirit of charity was purified as benefactor to the poor, only for his glory and not as I had spoiled before I left India my past charitable ventures by contaminating them with self-glory and self-gratification. He instilled in me slowly to empty the personal savings I earned in America for the sake of uplifting the poor and downtrodden people, in particular, the socially neglected seniors and abandoned children. Every time I forwarded some dollars to construct a few homes for this purpose and continued to spend on their food, dress, health, and education, I felt some indescribable joy, and whenever I visited those beneficiaries during my trips, I literally shed tears of joy seeing their happiness and salutations. Observing my ministry of charities, some of my parishioners in America came forward to add their donations, and with the blessing of Bishop Slattery, they were ready to collect as a second collection annually for this purpose during Christmas and Easter times. This, indeed, increased my joy.

Dasan: The same thing is true with me. I tried to support you with some donations I raised in my missionary life, and whenever I would go to those places and notice how amazingly they had been developed and how the residents were safe and sound, I felt great joy and continue to feel the same.

The Tears of Sorrow

Whoever is made to suffer as a Christian should not be ashamed but glorify God because of the name.

—1 Pet. 4:16

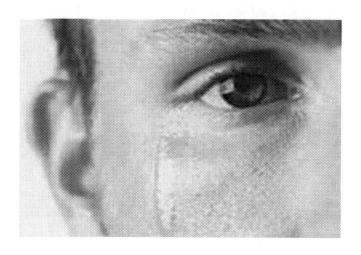

Ben: Before entering into the discussion on priestly tears of sorrow, let us remind ourselves of the inputs we both shared in the introduction of this book. The term *tears* is used here as only the outward signs and symbols of humans' feelings of joy, gratitude, excitement, wonder, awe, and grief or pain. As one author in his blog stated, "If weeping were a gesture with a single meaning, part of a universal language of feeling, then it would surely signify grief." That is the state with which it has been most frequently connected. In this meaning, we will be talking here about our tears, namely, our feelings of sorrow, pain, or agony, which we experience in our missionary commitments.

Dasan: I think both of us agree candidly on this holding. Definitely, the tears we discuss in this chapter are metaphors of the crosses we have been bearing in our priestly life and missionary works. All humans have our own sufferings and pains to be carried from womb to tomb. Jesus labeled all human sufferings as crosses. No Jew in the time of the Lord dared to use this term because it was a sign of degradation, death, crucifixion, criminal punishment, curse, and most horrific suffering.

Ben: Brother! Before sharing our experiences of sorrows in our missionary life, let us discuss a little about the reality of human sufferings and, specifically, our priestly tears.

Dasan: Suffering is an inevitable problem of humans. We believe God is perfect and infinitely good, but our mind shouts out, "Why is there so much suffering in his creation, and why is creation full of imperfections?

He could have avoided all sufferings and death! Look at nature: Big fish swallow small fish. Big animals kill small ones. Even a mother suffers giving birth to a baby. Does cruelty originate from God?"

The human mind wants to know everything by reason. But the reality of suffering is beyond human reason's grasp. Albert Einstein said, "*I don't believe in the laws of chance. I cannot believe that God plays dice with cosmos.*" So what I think is, we have to find an answer not from reason but elsewhere. We have to give up the idea that God always does what we think as good. We must accept God's ways are not our ways. But he is infinitely good, and we trust what he allows must be good and always for good.

Ben: I think no human born in this world, including the holiest, the greatest leaders and the most committed disciples of Jesus, are exempted from this treacherous dimension of life.

Dasan: Very true. For example, Pope Francis, all smiley leader of the twenty-first century, in one of his interviews with *Argentine Newspaper* on May 25, 2015, was asked whether he cries, and he said that he was moved by the sick, the suffering, and the imprisoned, which made him think that he could also be here. He too added, "*Publicly I do not cry. There were two occasions where I was at the limit, but I was able to stop on time. I was very much moved. There were even some tears that escaped, but I just played dumb and after wiped my hand on my face.*" Accepting his difficulty to bear physical pains, he was also quoted saying, "*Moral pain I can withstand, but physical, no. I am very cowardly when it* *comes to that. It's not that I'm afraid of an injection, but I prefer not to have problems with physical pain. I am very intolerant. I assume that it is something that stayed with me after a lung operation when I was nineteen years old."*

Ben: During my youth days, my frequent prayer to God was, "Never let me encounter any pain in my body." Later it was only an unanswered prayer. I began joining the crowd of humanity in most of my prayer times, asking God, "Where are you, God, in my time of sufferings?" and "Why have you done this to me?" But as you emphasized, through my meditation on his Word, as a second thought, immediately I tell the Lord, "Your will be done," because his Spirit clearly expresses in the scriptures, "*God did not make death, nor does he rejoice in the destruction of the living. For he fashioned all things that they might have being; and the creatures of the world are wholesome . . . But by the envy of the devil, death entered the world, and they who belong to his company experience it*" (Wis. 1:13–15). Therefore, God made us live, not die; God longed to see us living always in the Garden of Eden, where there were no tears or sorrows but only joy and peace. But according to the Book of Genesis, sin entered in the hearts of humans and destroyed all humans' wholeness and even disengaged the divine intention and dream about humans. Even those little deaths we face when we encounter illness—chronic and terminal and temporary sicknesses, like cold, stomachache, and the sufferings inflicted by our neighbors—are not from the hands of our Creator. As the Bible says, they are all the wages of our human sins.

Dasan: At the same time, we also should know that God does not want us to promote sufferings either; he wills that we should do our best to remove them and heal them. If nothing works out, accept them as the sign of our trust and fidelity to God. Besides, God desires we imitate Christ in transforming all our sufferings as sources of salvation both for ourselves and others. Paul underlines this Christian strategy in many of his letters. He writes: "*For you know the gracious act of our Lord Jesus Christ, that for your sake he became poor although he was rich, so that by his poverty you might become rich*" (2 Cor. 8:9). Naked and destitute on the cross, Jesus poured out his love on us. He even gave his life that we might have life. Quoting the prophecy of Isaiah, Peter beautifully describes how and why Christ handled his sufferings: "*When he was insulted, he returned no insult; when he suffered, he did not threaten; instead, he handed himself over to the one who judges justly. He himself bore our sins in his body upon the cross, so that, free from sin, we might live for righteousness. By his wounds you have been healed*" (1 Pet. 2:23–24).

Ben: Now let us share each other the tears of sorrow we shed in our ministries. Here I am sure neither do we glorify in our sufferings, nor do we mourn and groan to our readers or brag about how chivalrously we went through them. This is simply a very transparent exposition of both our humanity's ability and incapacity to face the consequences of our response to God's call of serving him as his missionaries in the world. Am I correct?

Dasan: You hit on something, Amalan! It is an irrefutable truth that God's call to become a missionary in his kingdom requires certain audacious faith, relentless hope, and undivided love toward him and his cause. As our joy can never become complete in this world but only perfected, so can our tolerance to sufferings only be perfected in a gradual process.

Ben: Some more things I want to insist from the very beginning of our conversation about our sufferings. We firmly hold any sorts of sufferings we list out here are not at all the works of God; we can also add this: The tears we shed due to the sufferings—which we refer as inflicted by our superiors, elders, relatives, friends, and common people—are not totally caused by them. First of all, the principal cause of the pains I felt and the tears I shed in my relationship with all my superiors and elders was mostly my impulsive and overambitious nature and not the political and diplomatic decisions taken by them. Secondly, about the conflicts I came across in my relationship with my fellow priests, if you interview them on this matter, they will testify that I behaved very exclusively, avoiding them because of my pride. They may be right. And my close relatives and friends also would agree with them. I had been so bent down to my success, progress, and fake self-prestige that I neglected these wonderful men and women and never shared with them my time, my love, and my concern. Thirdly, my view about sufferings was that I was bogged down from the side of ordinary people, whom I was sent to serve: Actually, I have to underscore those who caused me suffering were a minority. Later I will describe the terms *minority* and *majority* in this regard.

Dasan: I am so thrilled to hear your confession-like sharing of your well-balanced judgment on our sufferings. Electric power supply is made possible by the existence of two types of wires: positive and negative. Both are important to make bulbs light and other electric gadgets function. Similarly, painful or negative experiences help us grow in the acquisition of insight and maturity in life.

I have gone through experiences of criticism, correction, and failure. Though hurt, I have also been enabled to see some truth about which I had not been aware of all along. I have been challenged to be in contact with the whole truth of a given reality and to give up false beliefs about situations and, in the course of time, to drop altogether unreasonable expectations in life. One will never know what compassion is unless one has experienced pain and perhaps will never acquire the personal maturity.

Ben: Let me take the privilege of categorizing our crosses in missionary life and ministry under three headings. To be honest with you, this tagging is not mine; I borrow it from Pope Francis's homily at Chrism Mass in St. Peter's Basilica, April 2, 2015. Relating the priests' life and ministry to that of Jesus Christ's, the pope listed out our weariness as the "*weariness of ourselves,*" "*the weariness of people,*" and "*the weariness of enemies.*" Let us take the clue from the pope's words and, in a sort of far-fetched way, categorize our tears of sorrows as crosses we carry in our missionary life in three levels: Tears from carrying our own personal crosses, tears from bearing the crosses are that thrust upon us by our beneficiaries and benefactors, and thirdly, tears from enduring the crosses prodded on us by those (I won't call them enemies) who never liked us, whom we didn't like, and who hurt us because of their many limitations.

Let us first talk about the first kind of our sorrowful tears generated out of carrying our own personal crosses. Curious, I checked for a thousand one times the NT Books, where I would be reading Jesus's demand of his disciples carrying his cross and following him. He had never referred to his own cross; rather, he wanted us to carry our own crosses and follow him. Matthew quotes repeatedly, *"Whoever does not take up his cross and follow after me is not worthy of me"* (Matt. 10:38). Both Mark and Luke too follow Matthew, telling us Jesus desired that his followers must take up their own crosses and follow him (Mk. 8:34; Lk. 14:27).

Dasan: As the pope mentioned, this may be the most dangerous cross of all. That is because while the other two kinds come from being exposed, from going out of ourselves to anoint and to do battle, this kind of weariness is more "self-referential": it is dissatisfaction with oneself, but not the dissatisfaction of someone who directly confronts himself and serenely acknowledges his sinfulness and his need for God's mercy—his inability to cope with the burden of bitter choices one makes for his/her life.

Ben: More than any crosses, my self-inherited, self-imposed, self-derailed, and self-inflicted crosses have been the worst kind of sources that brought tears frequently. I have shared with you how my naive and spoiled-brat childhood life installed in my inner chamber so many in-line programs that were not fully realized, reasonably unreasonable, and that induced me to make the wrong choices

Dasan: Amalan! I chose to be a Jesuit priest. That means I had to live in a community and I had to fulfill my three vows—obedience to superiors, poverty both in spirit and material benefits, and lifelong celibacy. This sort of religious life commitment brought innumerable crosses, such as misunderstanding by others, subtle persecutions from my companions, and undeserved and unjust treatments by my superiors. Another kind of crosses came from those places and circumstances, which I hated to be in. Together with them all, I had to carry the yoke of feeling powerless. From that burden flowed the mental pain, loneliness, and lack of support, confusion and uncertainty, and meaningless happenings. I underwent tremendous bodily weakness and inertia when I strived to do my best to spread the Gospel.

It was very hard for me to gladly accept and obey some assignments given by my superiors, which might be unwanted and less glamorous. I too have suffered in belonging to the church with its tensions and divisions, and I continually suffer noticing the massive and overwhelming injustices in the world and, particularly, in India.

Ben: That is a very outspoken portrayal of your tears of sorrow shed in your religious community life. Let me share with you some of the crosses I had to carry in my personal priestly commitments.

On the day I was ordained as diocesan priest, with two vows of obedience and celibacy, as cranky as I always have been, I wanted to go beyond the achievements of all my colleagues by adding two more of my own commitments to God. One was the vow of poverty (readers must know that like my brother, Dasan, a religious priest, I, a diocesan priest, doesn't take this vow at our ordination), not only because I was attracted by Jesuits like you following exactly the evangelical discipleship demands of Master Jesus, but also my conscience was echoing every minute of the day the advice of our dad: *"My son, don't behave like other secular priests. They have a bad name among our villagers. There is a saying among our parishioners, 'Sending your son to be a diocesan priest means sending him to a foreign land to make money both for himself and for his family.'"*

Such a personal contract with God in choosing evangelical poverty made me so naive in managing my money, thinking that I wouldn't need it for my future because I firmly believed, besides my Creator, I was in the good hands of my bishop; hence, I didn't save anything at all from my limited income. Whatever came to my hands as personal savings, I used them on publishing my music books and discs or shared them with my friends and well-wishers. I too made sure not possessing any properties of my own except books bought for my home library. I used to tell proudly about myself to my parishioners that I don't need any vehicle to carry my properties as some of my fellow priests did;

I am not a catlike person who moves belongings from one parish to another, because I didn't own that much. I was a light traveler. However, in the recesses of my heart, I was shedding tears later when I felt the pinch of my poverty.

I never built any homes for my personal use. Even after I became fully committed to God's works in America, half of the dollars I get as my monthly salary are spent for my survival, and the other half, I save and forward to a few voluntary agencies in India to support my orphans and destitute seniors. If anything more is left, I use it for buying books and publishing books. Unfortunately, people around me never believed it; most of them, especially—I am vexed to mention this—my own relatives, were thinking I was a millionaire, the richest person in our area. More than the pinch of poverty, this kind of misunderstanding and gossip hurt me very much as a venomous sting. Till this day, I am shedding tears and bleeding in my heart.

Along with not hoarding money or property, my personal vow of poverty instructed me to deny any family ties. As our dad confirmed repeatedly in his advice sessions, our Master Jesus expects his committed disciples to detach themselves from their family relations—no strings attached. It had been my strategy to kill my enormous longing for being attached very loosely to my relatives. I made myself too busy in my ministries and distracted myself to ignore my family members, though they were residing in our hometown.

Dasan: Many times I too felt impotent to help in their basic needs even though I witnessed their deprivation. Especially, when I noticed our sister's utter poverty, my eyes were full of tears. I also was very much upset by her family problems. That was a big story. To summarize it, she was totally poor in its literal sense. The sufferings she and her family members underwent due to unemployment, hunger, and sickness were horrendous. Other people around her were interpreting this critical family situation as a kind of spell–result cast by her family's enemies or putting the blame on her husband and her own imprudent way of managing life. As for me, I was shedding tears every day in front of Jesus, asking him, "Why this?" even though there were two priests in our family dedicated to his missionary services. I am sure you had the same emotional disturbances; it might have been more than mine because our relatives were fully aware of my inability as a religious priest, but they would have expected from you more help as you are a diocesan (secular) priest.

Ben: Earlier I told you that I added personally two vows to the regular ones. Besides the promise of being poor, I gave my word to the Lord secretly that I would embrace any human being with no discrimination whatsoever. While the first three vows were very hard to practice, the last one was so easy to observe because of my naive personality, not having enough IQ to differentiate one human from another, except the difference of age and gender. I innocently thought every human is good and to be loved in the same way I loved my relatives. Unfortunately, as soon as I entered my diocese, I encountered the hateful rejection, not just from ordinary parishioners but among my fellow priests. In the name of caste, some group of priests belonging to a caste different from mine, excluded me from their company and not even held any conversation with me. On the other hand, some other senior priests invited me to their fellowship and treated me cordially as their brother and son. Unfortunately, they, later I came to know, were those belonging to my own caste. As much as possible, I tried to avoid such adherence to priests on the basis of caste similarity. Therefore, I became enemy to both caste-based factions. Moreover, as I was becoming more popular in my diocese and even in and around the region due to my successful music ministries, the priestly jealousy embedded with hatred put me in depression and acute pain. Physically and spiritually I was sick. I truly wanted to quit my profession and get away from all priestly functions. I was shedding tears of mental sorrows and psychological hurts.

Dasan: This takes us to the chat on the second kind of tears of sorrow we endure as priests. The pope very beautifully named it the weariness of people. It has been an amusing matter to observe the truth that almost all the people we have been sent to serve have been behaving strange, especially in their dealings with their priests.

Ben: I too found out this fact soon after my ordination, once I entered the crowd of people as a newly trained and groomed young man. Most of their behaviors seemed very strange, alien, and unlike from my own. In the beginning stage, though much perplexed and vexed, I pacified myself saying, "God put me in their midst to be a teacher, to be a model, and to be a prophet of change and renewal in their lives." While my emotional and intellectual energy was in high peak regarding those utopian but real ideals, my spiritual stamina was not that strong but only at its edge. Therefore, I lost my peace and became very restless whenever I came across the failures and fallouts of many of my congregational members and friends. I was in tears, which I consider now were simply the outcome of my immature spirituality, unbalanced personality, and unrealistic utopian mind-set.

Dasan: I like your self-introspection. We both must join the club of many other priests and missionaries who uselessly cry out for failures in realizing our idealistic dreams about our parishioners. Most of the time shedding tears in this situation is some sort of an outlet of our anger, our irritation, and emotional hurts, and is also a sign that we're forgetting the goodness of our God. He reiterates to all his priests in the scriptures that "*My hand shall ever abide with him, my arms also shall strengthen him*" (Ps. 89:21). It is also what our Father thinks whenever he "encounters" a priest. And he goes on to say, "*My faithfulness and my steadfast love shall be with him . . . He shall cry to me, 'You are my Father, my God and the rock of my salvation'*" (Ps. 89:24, 26). As the pope underlined in one of his homilies, "If the Lord is so concerned about helping us, it is because he knows that the task of anointing his faithful people is demanding; it can tire us. We experience this in so many ways: from the ordinary fatigue brought on by our daily apostolate to the weariness of sickness, death, and even martyrdom."

Ben: Pope Paul VI, in his encyclical *Evangelii Nuntiandi*, defines the concept of evangelization: It is a "process of bringing Good News into all the strata of humankind and, through its influence, transforming from within and making it new." He too emphasizes that the purpose of evangelization is the "interior change of the personal and collective consciousness of people, the activities in which they engage and the concrete milieu which are theirs."

From the day I was sent to be pastor for our people, I took to heart what Pope Paul wrote on evangelization; namely, I upheld the *interior change of the personal and collective consciousness of people* as the main motif for all my missionary works in whatever manner and style I could possibly undertake. I hold a firm belief that I have been sent by God for his purpose to various communities, thousands of individuals and groups of different caste, creed, denomination and race, though those happenings had been conspired and connived both by me and, surely, by my superiors.

On the day I arrived at any new service place, especially in America, first I preached to myself in private and then to my beneficiaries in public. This is how I worded it: *"As I start my ministry in your midst, my vision is very clear from the Lord. I am here to serve you as your animator and leader in your own witnessing Jesus, our God. As Jesus feels, we know there is so much to be done in this regard. The gifts are abundantly stored in Jesus's mansion. There are millions of people who hunger and search for those gifts. Only the laborers are few. Either they are absent or cold or indifferent or insensitive or in blissful ignorance and complacency. I hope you all will join with me in all possible ways to plan out new ways to implement*

Jesus's Harvest program in this place. First, let us implement it inside our parishes. I mean within our Catholic communities, let us introduce Jesus as the God of abundance. I shall be coming to you soon with various schemes. Please join me as laborers of Jesus in different ways. It can be through prayer, through offering talents and time and labor, and through monetary support."

That inner voice has been not that soft; it has been like the sound of thunder mixed with terrific lightning and very robustly hitting me in every heartbeat. Actually, it was a necessary but monstrous burden I had to carry within me through my life. Frequently it wearied me, tickled me, and bit me so painfully that many times my eyes were wet on two grounds: One, that inner noisy voice urging me to accomplish more and more and more programs and projects with no rest. The second one was that the more I implemented those projects seriously and very attentively, I couldn't see any results coming out of them; I was dismayed, depressed, and discouraged with my lack of achievements.

In addition to all this, most of the priests—religious and diocesan as well—follow very strictly certain norm in their homilies and talks freer of criticisms and to be always people-pleasing. Most of the Catholic preachers uphold a common coat of arms: "Be diplomatic and certainly be short." Here I mean that most of the priests make sure they don't question their congregation or challenge them in their discipleship requirements, and they too never speak anything that displeases their congregation and not to get their odium from them and, consequently, either lose them from parish roster or lose their big financial contribution. I found it hard to esteem my preaching ministry that way. While I was so thrilled and joyful and content during my meticulous and laborious undertakings in front of my people, at the end of them all, I felt empty, and in private, I was moved to tears of sadness. Because of continuous criticisms, or ill-willed comments, I paid a huge price of losing my sleep many nights.

Dasan: Amalan, I went through so many times the same critical situations of despair and despondency, at which I was thrown into a no-man's-land. I have to contend here that it was not so much the painful events that had affected me but my own way of perceiving them. This depended on my mind-set: beliefs, prejudices, conditionings, self-pity, wrong interpretations, and exaggerated fears. I had suffered more because of all these than because of actual painful situations I came across in my ministries. Hence, at one point, instead of lamenting over what I could not change, I began to focus on those that I could change. As William James has said, *"The great discovery of our times is that we can change our whole life by only changing the attitude of our minds."*

Ben: In my ministries, almost all my self-sufferings—physical, emotional, mental, and spiritual pain I felt—were the outcome of my imbalance encountered within my human spirit. It was a state of peacelessness, restlessness, and a loss of contentment. I confess I did shed tears in those times. Enlightened by various scriptures, I am aware of the various reasons for the human sufferings within me. The main cause is my sinfulness, which generates ignorance, pride, and stubbornness in making the wrong choices in life;

it induces to go for overdoses of bodily pleasures and uncontrolled emotions, leading to perversions and violations, and because of these, I suffer with ill health and social evils. However, at the end of the day, I must accept I am the total culprit. I had to reap its consequences. And not smilingly but with wounded pride, I was filled with tears of agony.

OK. Now let us turn to the second kind of sufferings we face that are generated by our people, among whom we were sent to preach the Good News.

Dasan: Brother, before we list out the hardships we experience in our dealings with our flock, we should be very clear about our Master's prophecies and promises whenever he plans to send us out on his mission, giving us a grand commission: *"Go, therefore, and make disciples of all nations, baptizing them in the name of the Father, and of the Son, and of the Holy Spirit, teaching them to observe all that I have commanded you."* And he too added a promise, *"Behold, I am with you always, until the end of the age"* (Matt. 28:19–20). He pointed out to us candidly to what kind of people he would be sending us to. Let me quote him: *"I am sending you like lambs among wolves"* (Lk. 10:3b). Like most of his hearers, he cautioned us that we too would face similar hard-hearted and hardheaded people in our ministries. Jesus said, *"Isaiah's prophecy is fulfilled in them, which says: 'You shall indeed hear but not understand. You shall indeed look but never see. Gross is the heart of this people, they will hardly hear with their ears, they have closed their eyes, lest they see with their eyes and hear with their ears and understand with their heart and be converted,"* but positively he too ended, saying, *"and I heal them"* (Matt. 13:14–15).

Ben: Yes, Dasan, I cherish in my heart always Jesus's encounter with his flock and his forbearing reaction and proaction toward such treacherous incidents and try my best to cope with mine. But one thing I have to emphasize here: In all my missionary placements arranged in the name of God but through both the weakness and strength of my superiors, whereas majority of humans brought in me tears of joy and gratitude and admiration, as I elaborated in the previous chapters, a minority of them were the cause of my sorrows, literally pain in all parts of my body and spirit. Some of them were good-willed people, compassionate and kind and forgiving and tolerating; they too were very honest and truthful. Many times a few among them didn't know how to communicate the truth that they think is "the truth" to me; even I explained to them the reason for my different view in a very amicable and friendly way, because of their stubborn and unbending mind-set (I used to tease them the redheaded) to listen to what I would say to them; despite my admiration for their sharp, outspoken behavior, many times I was drowned in troubled waters crying aloud in my privacy, "O holy terrorists!"

Dasan: I did meet rejection and misunderstanding and mudslinging from the people whom I was serving as teacher, guide, preacher, writer, and organizer. I don't think I felt as much heat and hurt during those moments as you would have been for the main reason I stated earlier: I was experiencing such things in my own community life. Maybe I actually became "rejection proof" to confront them outside in the parishes or education environment.

Ben: I confirm what I had said earlier: One of my problems in my pastoral and spiritual efforts throughout my missionary life has been how humanity, specifically the frantic power-mongers and their supporters, misunderstand the activities performed by crusaders of change and renewal around the globe. Many a time the Spirit-led and Spirit-involved efforts of purifying and renewing religious and political systems, such as writing, speaking, and conducting forums and conferences, have been contemplated as conspiracies relating to sedition, rebellion, or coup d'état. This has been a continuous tears-generating source from the outset of priestly ministry.

Secondly, let me elaborate how the element of people's rejection affected my missionary spirit. I did explain what kind of rejection I dealt with while I was serving the people of Tamil Nadu. The more I became popular in public, particularly by my application of arts and media with incongruous blending of the Catholic priestly status and the role of performing theatrical artist. That was too much for both the leaders and ordinary people to digest. They judged it was impossible; therefore, either they scorned me as an impure person unfit to put on the priestly robe, or they avoided me and my efforts as bad as the "snake drama" at the Garden of Eden. Such a callous and very naive attitude killed my interest and my sincerity of purpose. I cried and cried in private; I couldn't weep to anybody because there was nobody who would possess a magnanimous heart.

Dasan: Amalan! When I visited you once while you were serving as pastor in one American parish, you had shared with me about the "trail of tears"—that was how you named it—you have been undergoing. You said that while you were studying and serving as priest in Eastern Oklahoma, you expected to taste the same freedom and love you had experienced in Chicago some fifteen years ago. It was a big shock for me to hear that you were disappointed in this matter and felt very sad about it. Except your bishop and a few priests in the diocese, many never welcomed you, and though you tried to befriend them, they had ignored you and avoided you.

Ben: Rightly so. There might have been many other human reasons for such harsh dealings. What I want to highlight here are the following: First, there was an age-old inborn intolerance for new immigrants, colored ones in particular. I was very apprehensive to notice the deliberate discrimination and rejection of me as I had already lived through in India, due to casteism. I had to put up with this sort of discrimination and disliking and suspecting mind-set even among some of my parishioners. Though I was shedding tears frequently during my minutes with my Master, I never missed instructing them the right path of justice and love that Jesus has shown to us. Historically, racial problem is a perennial one in the States. In a convincing manner, I have been preaching to them, saying, "We are not African-Americans. We are not Asian-Americans. We are not Indian-Americans. I'm tired of all the hyphenated Americans. We are only Americans."

What I meant was whether they are parents or grandparents or great-grandparents who came from various parts of the globe as pilgrims, immigrants,

migrants, or refugees or anyone who has been legally naturalized with full citizenship and job opportunity, all are to be recognized only as Americans and not branded as culturally correct labels.

I went further and added that in the country that is made one under God, every human who begins to survive and live his/her dream in America the Beautiful is respected as the child of the same God who offers rain as well as makes the sun shine on all humans with no discrimination. America is not simply a melting pot or a rainbow but a true heaven on earth. It is like a Noah's ark in which both the educated and the uneducated, the poor and the rich, the young and the old, the runners and the winners, and the first and the last find a safety network in the bond of Christian love as if it were a new heaven and a new earth.

Dasan: The discrimination of foreigners—in any form, shape, or status—is a common factor around the globe. While I was in Britain or Malaysia, I too had to put up with it. Yes, in one way, we can tolerate it as a human thing. But as you said, as messengers of God, we have been sent to those places to convert or, as Pope Francis always says, to evangelize our own Catholic people the Gospel values of love.

Ben: Yes, brother, that was how I envisioned my life and my parishioners' and priest friends' lives were supposed to be. Being the first colored foreign priest serving in the diocese, I had to put up with the unchristian attitude of priests and laity. However, with the help and counseling of my close friends in the diocese and because of my gray and golden wisdom of retreating, I managed my life both going with the flow serenely and swimming against the current with boldness. Gradually, except a few, all Catholic parishioners whom I served became friendly to me.

Dasan: Here I am tempted to ask you one big question. While you were sadly disappointed by the treatment of Americans, though a few in number, how did you decide to become incardinated to an American diocese and to be naturalized as American citizen?

Ben: Very good question, brother. Let me answer to you. While I was serving in America as an Indian missionary propelled by God's will, I felt I was thrown into an exile that most of the third-world countrymen have been esteeming as a land of opportunities where milk and honey overflows, as the biblical promised land. And in a way, it was true; this is why my relatives and friends in India perceived me as the richest man of their clout and one priest enjoying uninterrupted pleasure, entertainment, and freelance "hickory pickery" overdose of his independence to the brim. This misunderstanding made me psychologically sick. On the contrary, I encountered completely a lonely man in the midst of a variable, vulnerable, and vindictive crowd. My tears of sorrows at this were not so much of the absence of my beloved relatives and friends in India or of the absence of love and support from my American counterparts and laity, but unmistakably, my tears welled up because of the disappointment I felt when I went through the same hatred, jealousy, coldness, suspicion, discrimination, and strongly inhibited prejudices in the States as I endured in India. You may say all men are equal in this, but personally, I had high-rated dreams about my beloved America, a God's country, where freedom and justice are the main wheelers of the social systems.

Through my higher studies in this country, I had been drinking and tasting the greatness and sweetness of the American spirit of freedom and justice. When I went back to India, I was actually walking in the clouds of such utopian dreams to bring change and renewal among my fellow countrymen. As we conversed earlier, I rode that Hercules horse with fairy wings for almost fifteen years. You know, I failed. When I came back to America, I wanted to feel the fresh air of the same Americanism and become more vibrant to fly high with my unceasing dreams. However, as I told you, I was disappointed. That was the big blow for me; I sensed so many slaps hitting on my face. Though such was the story of my tears of sorrows in the beginning years of my ministry in America, the local bishop and some parishioners who joined with me as my best friends induced me to stay back. On the part of the bishop, I knew it was only because I was needed to fill in the vacant parishes, but on the part of my lay friends, they inspired me that the people of this region needed my spiritual presence and ministry more than the people in India.

This is because they had heard and read almost all my homilies and articles to my audiences inside the church as well as in other public events, exposing the shortfall in the development and civilization of today's society, especially the lack of honesty, justice, and unity in India and other parts of the third world, whereas in America, I was concentrating on the spiritual fervor and the need of intimate relationship not just with the religion but mostly with God the Almighty. Since I was repeating this message on a regular basis, I didn't get the kind of universal accolades as many as I garnered in the field of arts. However, an elite group of Oklahomans joined me as godsent friends encouraging me. Yes, it was nothing but God's work. Finally, I consented to stay back in America once and for all.

Dasan: Rights to believe or not to believe are both valid and treasured positions of a free people. While in most part of the world many people adhere to religions either superstitiously or emotionally, as far as I know, I am sure you too would agree with me, Westerners, in general, who choose to be religious take it very genuinely and commit to Jesus's Gospel as best as they can.

Ben: Wholeheartedly, I am of the same opinion, and that is why America is very close to my heart, besides my mother India. From the years I spent in Chicago filling my brain with American dreams and its democratic ideas about humanity, I developed an admiration and awe toward it, the truly God's country. As one author puts it, *"America the Beautiful is one of the few largest civic nations because it is founded, as Jefferson said, on 'truths' deemed 'self-evident,' and committed, as Abraham Lincoln put it, to a vision 'that all are created equal.'"* It is a known fact that Americans take religion very seriously. One Catholic confessed her plight and flight in shopping around for, as she verbalized, *wandering for God*, in her article in one of the Catholic magazines. I am quoting her: "*I have been to at least twenty churches, worship services and communities in the last four years. Since I moved back to the Bay Area in 2011, I have been guilty of going to one church because I resonate with their homilies, another church because I deeply connect with the music, another because I enjoy their faith-sharing groups, and yet another because I experience their efforts of inclusion in a positive way. I, like many in this young adult generation, roam around each Sunday in search for the most complete, authentic experience of community*" (NCR Mar. 13, 2015). She is absolutely correct in emphasizing how not only youngsters but also seniors in most of the parishes in Western countries have become the spiritual seekers.

I entered America at a time of profound demographic shift as Hispanics, Asians, Africans, Caribbean people, and many other communities of non-European origin had been on the rise. I too was encouraged to read in the recent report of USCCB's Committee of Cultural Diversity in the Church about what our Roman Catholic Church in the United States thinks about this cultural diversity. While accepting the mission of the today's church to proclaim the Gospel of Jesus Christ and promote the life and dignity of each and every human being had much to do with insight into cultures, the committee also recommended that "for ministers and pastoral workers to be effective in this diverse environment, the right knowledge, attitudes, and skills needed to be developed." I thought that God called me through my bishop friend at the right time to serve as a missionary in his diocese, when, according to the statistics taken by research centers, the number of priests available for active duty in American parishes continued to drop and the result was an increase in the number of parishes without a resident pastor.

Dasan: I was aware of this critical situation not only in America but in the global church also. Many dioceses in the States, as I heard and read, have been trying to make up for the declining number of priests by bringing in priests from other countries to minister in parishes. It is a very surprising news that the number of "international priests" has more than doubled over the past fifteen years, from about 3,500 in 1999 to close to seven thousand today. These priests come from India, the Philippines, Nigeria, Mexico, and other countries and commit to serve in US parishes so that bishops do not have to close or merge existing parishes. Isn't that right?

Ben: Though God pushed me into this American life because of the in-dire-need situation of his church, personally, regrettably, I admit it was not my sole concern. You know well, from my childhood, I spurned to be enslaved by inferiority complex. That was mostly due to my mom's uninterrupted, lovable cuddling and my snuggling into her admiration for me in my babyhood: "You are my prince, baby." In addition to it, living in and breathing American culture, I seemed to swallow without thinking the culture of success at all costs. I heard and watched almost all leaders in politics and religion in the States chanting, "Go, go, go! Win, win, win! Be beautiful! Be successful! Be great! Be powerful! Positive thinking! Beat the other guy! You can do it!" Some writer called it "the alpha American achievement culture." Since I had already such "go beyond" spirit in me, this alpha culture attracted me very much.

Dasan: Brother! It seems to me this kind of mind-set is a little too exhausting, and from a Catholic point of view, it doesn't really fit with Gospel values. Even though Paul, being a chivalrous and a very sportive person, writes in his letters his life's initiatives and enterprises as "running the race, fighting the good fight, finishing the course, and winning the prize," there is also the theme of taking up our cross and discovering the paradoxical truth that God's glory is revealed not in strength but in weakness.

Ben: I fully concede to what you underlined. As most of baby boomers', most of my moves in priestly life had been based on wrongly misinterpreting Paul and other positive thinkers and uncritically accepting the alpha American achievement culture. With no reservation, I testify the end result of all this was shedding tears of depression, anguish, dissatisfaction, and peacelessness. It took for me so many years to recant such view about life! Now let us turn to the difficulties in dealing with our superiors.

Dasan: Earlier I described the undeserved and unjust treatments by superiors was one of my crosses to bear in priestly life. As a Jesuit, follower of St. Ignatius, the leader of our congregation learned from the years of novitiate, "*We must put aside all judgment of our own and keep the mind ever ready and prompt to obey in all things the true Spouse of Christ our Lord, our holy Mother, the hierarchical Church.*" As our founder advised, I have tried my best to keep on obeying my superiors as seeing God in them and being assured that obedience is the safest guide and most faithful interpreter of the Divine Will.

When I grew up and acquired a standing position and role in the society, I pondered a lot on the pros and cons of the so-called blind obedience. Senior priests like me find it hard even to discuss on this debatable subject; the young brother priests have gone ahead of me in this matter. While I found it hard to obey the orders that came out of biased attitudes, unjust conclusion about my behavior and action, my trained Jesuit heart was propelling me to obey them. Many times you even indicated about my habit of sharing my thoughts and suggestions to my superiors for any life or ministry decisions but always adding as closing remark at the end of my letters my full-hearted obeisance to their discretion. That is the way I had been formed, and that is the way I continue till my last breath despite the bleeding within me.

Ben: I am very sorry, brother, for the sarcastic comments I threw at your positive and holistic spiritual approach on religious obedience. Let me describe my relations with my elders and superiors. Undoubtedly, almost all my elders and superiors did everything in and for my life out of their goodwill and faith and a certain filial and brotherly responsibility over my vocation and ministry. Unfortunately, I have to confess here, some of them did so much harm to me because of their wrong impression, twisted conviction, and a bit of jealousy. I shared with you how our wonderful parents and siblings acted or reacted in my life's choices, how my superiors in the seminary judged me as girlish boy, useless to nothing, and how badly I was treated by superiors and elders during my ministries both in India and in America. Actually, they were all thinking they were doing justice to their leadership and accountability to the people and the Almighty. Behind their back, they carried a large amount of personal agenda whenever they dictated me to obey them.

Here are just some examples: While I was working in my native diocese as a committed disciple of Jesus in communication field, one day, that was after nearly fourteen years of service to the diocese and Tamil-speaking people, I thought I was in great spiritual crisis and wanted to get a break from 24-7 hard labor. I didn't even want to go for a pleasure trip or vacation; rather, I proposed to my superior that I wanted to go for a sabbatical and equip myself and renew my spirit and skills more to be of greater use to God and the church. Very sadly my superior was not happy with my request, but he couldn't resist it, because from the bottom of his heart, he knew I needed it. However, in order to threaten me and thus to ignore my request, he said to me, "If you go, you cannot return to Sathangai Communication Center," which you know was my brainchild. That kind of attitude hurt me very much; for days I was in tears. Nonetheless, I said okay to his decision and got his permission to go to America for my sabbatical.

Dasan: Was there any of this hurting incident that occurred to you while you were serving in America? I am sure you will agree with me your superior in the diocese where you joined has been your personal friend.

Ben: Absolutely, he was, he is, and he will be my one and only personal friend who is also my superior. You know friends can inflict sometimes horrible wounds. My superior, as I professed in the previous chapter, has done wonderful things for me. There is no doubt about it. I too have acknowledged this publicly in one of my books recently published, saying I dedicate it to him, "*who entered in the middle of my priestly life as a docile Catholic priest and taught me how to live single-mindedly in priestly spirituality, and as a bishop, he guided me to find my right life situation with Christ and settle in it and rest.*" Nevertheless, I have to reveal to you this. I was acutely hurt by him because he was my close friend, who, I thought, would understand the difficulties and struggles I was undergoing because one, he publicly declared we both were longtime friends (which surely made other diocesan priests feel jealous and afraid to make contacts with me wrongly, judging I might be an informant to the superior) and two, he didn't enjoy listening to my personal sharing of joy and sorrow in the ministry, which I did imprudently on a regular basis. Naturally, he wanted to be peaceful in his role as bishop and found it as a healthy approach. I tried my best to continue my music ministry in America; I published five new books written by me at the auspicious Year of Faith—all in English! He never encouraged me, nor did he endorse my communication works. God only knows why he didn't! This wounded my inner spirit.

A time came I was swirled into my ministerial life's edge. I requested him to permit me to retire even though I had not reached my regular retirement age. With no dialogue, he accepted it. He would have forgotten what I personally told him about my wish a few months earlier. I had expressed to him of my desire to continue my active ministry as long as I was healthy if I were to be assigned in a more energetic and larger community. I might have been wrong, but I did request it of him; I didn't mention this in my retirement request letter.

Let us now focus on some more problems we face as missionaries while we serve the community members.

Dasan: Recently I came across a global survey on the life and ministry of international priests, especially those serving in America. In it I read the compiler of that report listing out some critical issues American Catholics shared. Among them, the most excruciating remarks against the foreign missionaries (international priests) like us, are the following: they are limited and unable in communicating in the local English, and they don't know the local culture of America.

Ben: Debate on the (missionary priests) international priests' arrival and ministry in the United States is an ongoing event. Those who are debating about the influx of the international priests to America place some problematic criticisms, which are almost like those thrown against the outsourcing efforts in the commercial world.

Dasan: Catholics in America, as some magazines emphasized, prefer American priests over international priests, and the main reason is language and empathy. They also corrected themselves, noting that not all Catholics feel this way. Some cosmopolitan laypersons felt conflicted and a bit embarrassed when they talked about this, saying that they wished American laity were more receptive to priests from all nations and cultures, but the reality is that most laity are not. Only in certain parishes would laypeople welcome an international priest as much as an American.

Ben: Very sadly, the reporters in magazines and in books hold an extreme contention that foreign-born priests bring problems in the parishes because of the following: untrained in spoken American English, cultural misunderstandings, different ecclesiology, finances and fund-raising, and aversion to mixing with other priests. I have no qualm to agree fully with the survey that language is the main problem, namely, no perfect command in communicating in English. However, my question from the start of my ministry in America has been this: what kind of English? Colloquial? Regional? Urban? Rural? American? British? Asian? Northwest or Southcentral? Baptist or Pentecostal? Youth or old? Already there are hundreds of usages of the English language, spoken and written, around the globe. It is a known fact that one, in his/her acquaintance with another person, has to patiently deal with this linguistic problem if a human truly wants to maintain logical and humane relationships. As a communication student, I heard from my Chicago communication professors it takes time to reach the high peak of communication between communicator and receiver as well. At the onset of my life journey, it took for me six months to understand professors, superiors, and surely parishioners. Most of the time, except the professors, I found no grammar in spoken English, as it is common in all the languages of the world. Hence, communication between a foreign missionary and the local parishioners is, as one veteran female lay minister is quoted saying in the survey, "never going to be perfect." But still, I wept for my inability to cope with this problem every day.

Dasan: Tell me, Amalan, how did you cope with the incendiary comments tossed at your preaching ministry by your parishioners and, surely, by many American priests?

Ben: Though a foreign-born American citizen, living and working as pastor and preacher in the States for more than twenty years, I find it hard to reach out to my parishioners with my heartfelt messages of the Gospel of Jesus, effectively and fruitfully. I am a communication student. I have gone through a special course, even in speech communication. However, I still fall short of using suitable and proper accent peculiar to Americans, especially the Americans in Eastern Oklahoma. As many of my international priest friends have shared with me, I too experience the same disappointment and feel sad when I hear some of the congregational members remarking, "Father, we could not understand you." In my communication studies in Chicago, my professor used to encourage me not to fall victim to some bogus audience that always threatens any public speaker. He indicated that according to an audience research, while 25 percent of the audience would be hostile and the other 25 percent indifferent, the remaining 50 percent will always be on the side of the speaker. So he advised me to focus my whole attention on the favorable portion of the audience in every one of my public speeches.

Nonetheless, in the light of my communication tactics, I discovered in my church congregations three groups of audiences with some different equation: 10 percent of them disliked me; either they didn't attend my Mass or went to some other church and dropped attending the events and programs happening in my parish. There was another group of audience (10 percent) who never cared for a theologically oriented or biblically founded preaching from any of their pastors; a few among them might have listened to me when I made some funny jokes or related anecdotes or gave out some startling views on any burning issues or made some interesting announcements about some current activities in the community. Indeed, they behaved like timekeepers in the sense they kept looking at their wristwatches every five minutes as their ticking or tickling as their hearts did! After five minutes of listening, all their senses automatically stopped cooperating.

Another 10 percent of my hearers, because of their disabled hearing sensitivity, could not listen to the speaker properly. This kind of hard-to-hear situation would have been caused either by old age or by regular listening to noisy sound through the environment or modern audio technology or by psychological problem created by their prejudices against strangeness or newness around their lives.

The rest of the 70 percent of the parish congregation are true and sincere audience who, even though the voice and accent they hear and the appearance of a person they see seems a little difficult to cope with, try to listen and understand what their pastor wants to convey to them. These parishioners come every Sunday to their church not attracted by the loveliness, the colorfulness, and the smartness of their pastor. Their main purpose in participating in the church service is to worship their Lord, to feel his nearness and that of their fellow parishioners; above all, they are led by the Spirit who dwells in them. They consider the Sunday worship as a sacred family obligation for listening to their God, for communing with him in the Eucharist, and for lifting up their thanks and petitions for every fellowman in and around their lives. It is this group I concentrated on and did my best to reach out to with my in-depth spiritual sharing.

As my professor advised, I started being least bothered about those 30 percent of the flock who would leave and reject me because of their biased attitudes and spiritual limitations, but I would always pray and wait for their return home.

I paid then more attention to my favorable audience in my preaching duty. After every Mass while I hugged everyone who attended Sunday worship and showed my love and respect, I attentively listened to the feedback of those 70 percent of my congregation. They were the true critics of my preaching. I loved preaching not only as my priestly duty but as my life, as my vocation, and as a prophetic call of God from heaven. Over the years, my lovable and grace-filled audience have offered me many criticisms, some sharp, bitter, and hurting. That is part of the gifts I am expected to receive from my people. Of course, I had had enough criticisms from my professors and fellow students in communication classes. Yet I love to hear from my own parish audience in person.

Among this adorable audience, I know fully well a few still find it hard to understand me. Therefore, with a heavy heart and tears of sorrow, I have been trying hard to reach out to my God-given people and feed them spiritual food of the Word of God through various means. I was publishing every Sunday my homily notes in the form of a bulletin letter so that the audience could take it and read once again at home and reflect over what they had heard on that Sunday. In addition, I strained myself to publish a book compiling my own Sunday homilies for all three liturgical years and handed out to them, for it would be more useful to them if they had read my homily notes before they came to church, and consequently, they would understand me better.

Dasan: I admire at you, Amalan, on this matter. I read one person in the survey I read admitting that "*Indian priests like us are difficult, and they're the deepest. They seem to have a rich sense of spirituality, but it really is difficult. You have to listen hard.*" This also is true in my ministry in England. It was so hard for me to "liquidate" Jesus's Gospel of spiritual values for the sake of some people who, in another survey I read, are shopping around for the right preachers who sell prosperity Gospel, for a pleasing and flexible minister, and for a parish accommodating and socializing religion. First of all, Christ's values are hard to even listen to—worse still if they are preached by foreigners who are very much different from their mind-set, soul, skin, and others.

Ben: Here let me share a bit more of my thoughts on this issue of people's rejection on the basis of my language. All that I accomplished over those years were mostly centered on mass communication within the purview of the media, such as theater, print, celluloid, and electronic as well. While I was engaged in those media services, I always esteemed, endorsed, used, and taught interpersonal communication technique as the source and basis for any effective human communication. I emphasized person-to-person contact as the most powerful and credible technique in the field of development communication. However, while I gave priority to one-to-one communication in my teaching and theorizing, I actually was not involved much in it. I tried my best to build up rapport between me and the American Catholics and their priests. I honestly say I failed in interpersonal communication, for which many of them would blame on my lack of fluency in American language. Being trained in communication techniques at Chicago universities, I find that any survey or research or any religious right-wing writers' criticism is not new at all, because I knew my limitations from the beginning of my missionary life in America, especially the region I was called to serve God and the church. I learned the so-called American English while I was studying and serving in Chicago and Brooklyn, where the style of spoken English was very fast, very punctuating, and very grammatical. But English spoken in the region I served as pastor was very slow, broken, poetic, and with a sort of tinny flute tone. When I entered this territory, I was already past my middle age, but still I tried my best to learn speaking in slow pace and tried harder to imitate a regional kind of talking. You know, I failed indeed. It was too much for me at that age. My superior encouraged me, as he did all my colleagues who reported about their communication problems.

Though there is a little bit of truth in the debates on the presence and ministry of the international priests, I cannot accept the entire findings as genuine, primarily because many such surveys have been conducted among a very tiny minority of American Catholics. Even in their responses, some have added the worth of having these missionaries of modern time.

Dasan: Now explain about the second criticism on the cultural misunderstanding pitched against international priests.

Ben: Regarding this unjustified criticism, I have to say this from my experience in the States: No priest, young or old in this modern-media world, is exempted in the know of what sort of culture he is entering. America has been an open book that has been read, seen, heard, punctured, publicized, and thrown overboard by some, but most of the global family love it for its enterprising and entrepreneurial glory in this twenty-first century.

The critics point out that we, the foreign priests, don't know how to deal with women. My only question is, how far does a Catholic priest under the sky do that perfectly? Invariably every Catholic priest, being trained and groomed in a weird administrative system, comes out of the seminary with a sense of the priest as superior, and that causes a lot of tension.

So it is wrong to say just us who come from different countries are culpable of such "macho" idea, as I name it, or superiority complex; those issues are all out there inside the global network of the Catholic Church, sometimes subtle and sometimes blatant. I too must confess this: I have watched and heard many women of the parishes I served telling me how they were neglected by American priests themselves.

Barbara Parsons, an American Catholic writer, decrying the common "spiritual assault" of certain American priests, namely, their moral nonsense, scriptural distortion, historical inaccuracy, and theological make-believe in their practices and homilies, wrote in her article (*Commonweal* 2-19-15) that one of her priests, who was in his thirties, had proclaimed, in three respective sermons: "Men should govern women"; "You cannot love yourself"; and "The Catholic Church has always supported science." The same man, moreover, informed all of us nonordained folks at a pastoral council meeting that when a priest dies and enters heaven, "he goes to a higher place in heaven than laity do." Finally, at the beginning of Lent, both priests signed a letter, distributed in both parishes, advising us "to remember that all suffering is a gift from God."

Undoubtedly, a minority group of priests, of any race or skin, inside the Catholic Church, do hurt the pure and simple faith of ordinary parishioners. Also, I ask those critics: Have you taken a survey on how many of us, balanced as we are, rely largely on groups of women in every parish, both in our native land and in the land we come to serve? Personally, I never grudged accepting a woman, like a woman on the staff, as an equal. Almost all my life as seminarian, priest, and missionary messenger, after my mom, I depended on women more than men for my ministries and projects. It is horrendous to hear some mudslingers throw stone at missionary priests that culturally they look at women very, very differently. I don't weep for their remarks but only for their prejudiced attitude and hatred that foams out in this manner.

There is one more criticism lodged against missionary priests, very serious and very close to Catholic values. I read someone telling the interviewer that these men don't understand our culture, particularly when it comes to marriage. Priests coming from different parts of the world, though they are born and bred in a culture of arranged marriages, are fully aware of the modern decadence of Christian marriage not only in the Western world but also in all continents. I myself, in the beginning, did feel some shock waves passing through my Catholic mind and body (because I am a cradle Catholic) when I faced issues like the lifestyle of living together or free in sexual mores, like premarital sex and, of course, the whole fight between two extreme ideologies of pro-choice and pro-life. Intelligent as we are, we immediately refer to our superiors, especially the marriage tribunal in charge, on any matter that bothered me as the deviations from the Catholic culture.

Dasan: I regret, Amalan, how those who reject us out of self-centered motives can go to the extreme of silly criticisms like this. I did feel like you and other foreign missionaries in the beginning of my ministry, "I've come here to save the Western Catholic Church, because it's going down the drain!" In later years, I understood as blessed John Paul II used to say, "With God we have to patiently but fervently face this culture of death." This must be included as another dimension of our sorrows.

Ben: In this prolonged debate on the validity of bringing missionary priests from foreign land, except a few references here and there by some good-willed and well-balanced Catholic writers and speakers, almost all remarks they have been alluding to as scaring problems presented by these modern missionaries, avoided the subtle and intertwined reasons some of our priests and people show their apprehension against missionary (international) priests. Let me list a few:

1. Rejection because of racial attitude.
2. Rejection because of the colored skin: *White Americans never like colored priests perform theirs or their children's weddings, but they welcome them to administer other sacraments, especially the last rite and even burial ceremonies.*
3. Rejection because of the aversion for hard English (King's or Queen's) accent—regarding my failure in reaching out to my congregations through my homilies and talks.
4. Rejection because of misunderstanding about the living standard of India and other third-world countries.

5. Rejection because of misinterpretation of my coming to America to hoard wealth.
6. Rejection due to holding certain myths about Indian attitude, for example, that all Indian males treat women as their slaves.
7. Rejection because of the wrong perception that every foreign priest is fully ignorant of American situation.

Dasan: Well said, Amalan. Any spiritually well-groomed person would agree to your list. This doesn't mean in any way we belittle the limitations of ours and other missionary (international) priests. We are what we are, and so all the priests are of any origin, race, and color. I too admit while I was hurt by this intolerant and unchristian approach to the presence of these missionaries, I and other missionaries, having grown up in Jesus's stature, never quit our response to the call of the Almighty.

Ben: Truly tears are flowing from our eyes and bleeding in our inner sanctuary. However, this does not denote that we want to be losers. We have risen up and walked. We fought the good fight as Paul did. As our Master Jesus, we always go beyond, which Pope Francis reminded using an Italian term at the onset of his pontificate: *Avanti.*

Dasan: As a final note to this chapter, allow me, Amalan, to quote from *Evangelii Gaudium*, which is supposed to be the spirit behind the ministries performed by all modern Catholic missionaries in fire and dungeon: "*Those who by God's grace accept the mission, are called to live* *the mission. For them, the proclamation of Christ in the many peripheries of the world becomes their way of following him, one which more than repays them for the many difficulties and sacrifices they make. Any tendency to deviate from this vocation, even if motivated by noble reasons due to countless pastoral, ecclesial or humanitarian needs, is not consistent with the Lord's call to be personally at the service of the Gospel.*

The missionary dimension, which belongs to the very nature of the Church, is also intrinsic to all forms of consecrated life, and cannot be neglected without detracting from and disfiguring its charism. Being a missionary is not about proselytizing or mere strategy; mission is part of the 'grammar' of faith, something essential for those who listen to the voice of the Spirit who whispers 'Come' and 'Go forth.' Those who follow Christ cannot fail to be missionaries, for they know that Jesus 'walks with them, speaks to them and breathes with them. They sense Jesus alive with them in the midst of the missionary enterprise.'"

The End Results of Priestly Tears

Those who sow in tears will reap with cries of joy.

—Ps. 126:5

Dasan: In conclusion of the discussion we, the missionary priest brothers held in this book, want to expose to our readers what we gain from our shedding of all these kinds of tears. We explained clearly in every chapter the causes of those tears. While the tears of gratitude and joy come out of wonder, awe, and excitement, those of sorrow are secreted by awareness of one's inabilities, remorse of conscience, and physical and emotional pain and agony.

Ben: Nonetheless, a valid question can be posted by modern pragmatic people: where do all these tears lead us to? One writer in his blog very sarcastically responds that all tears free humans from their tension, like, for example, urinating. Another author goes a little further to underline that all liberating tears are some sort of masturbating. Theater students like me learned in our theater classes that one of the effects of theater performances is a cathartic experience, which releases the spectators from their emotional and intellectual spasms. What I and my brother have to underscore is that the effects of our priestly tears are much deeper and higher than all the above-listed results. It is because we enlisted and well described the origin and process of the shedding of those priestly tears, which are, though humanity-based, closely and intrinsically connected to God's kingdom. Therefore, their end also must be related to God.

Dasan: Unquestionably, that is correct. In this regard, let us quote some of God's words on the results of our tears: First of all, a faith-filled priest firmly upholds with the psalmist that "*Lord, my wanderings you have noted; are* *my tears not stored in your flask, recorded in your book?"* (Ps. 56:9) and that *"Those who sow in tears will reap with cries of joy"* (Ps. 126:5). According to the Book of Revelation, *"God will wipe every tear from their eyes, and there shall be no more death or mourning, wailing or pain, [for] the old order has passed away"* (Rev. 21:4). In faith, every priest, as they are on his knees, asks their Master in tears with Peter, *"We have given up everything and followed you."* We know what he wanted to ask, but Jesus, who knew his mind, responded immediately, *"Amen, I say to you, there is no one who has given up house or brothers or sisters or mother or father or children or lands for my sake and for the sake of the gospel who will not receive a hundred times more now in this present age: houses and brothers and sisters and mothers and children and lands, with persecutions, and eternal life in the age to come"* (Mk. 10:28–30). Those words of our Master are always ringing in our prayer cell.

Jesus also said, *"I have observed Satan fall like lightning from the sky. Behold, I have given you the power 'to tread upon serpents' and scorpions and upon the full force of the enemy and nothing will harm you. Nevertheless, do not rejoice because the spirits are subject to you, but rejoice because your names are written in heaven"* (Lk. 10:18–20).

Ben: As Jesus's disciples, we believe that he, the Son of that God of abundance, set his life goal as to offer abundant life to us. He says, *"I came so that they may have life and have it more abundantly."* Since it's this God we work for in whatever life situation and it is this God of abundance we introduce and proclaim to our communities, we don't rely on small and puny contentment; rather, we aim for a very big reward from his hands. We are surrounded by a society that is costing its lot for abundance in different harmful ways. The world is truly in search of a God of abundance. It has not seen him or felt him. We are to be blamed for it, because Jesus entrusted that task to us to go and introduce his God to the world, and we have not done it sufficiently. Our world needs now more than ever before such hometown witnesses for Christ. We, the missionary priests, are such witnesses, and paying heed to the Master's clarion call, we encourage and form the future witnesses too. *"The harvest is abundant but the laborers are few; so ask the master of the harvest to send out laborers for his harvest"* (Lk. 10:2). Our tears in any form in no way should hinder this perennial vocation from God and his Beloved Son.

Dasan: Pope Francis, in his homily at the canonization Mass of St. Joseph Vaz in Colombo, Sri Lanka, 1-14-15, said, *"Saint Joseph Vaz gives us an example of missionary zeal. Though he came to Ceylon to minister to the Catholic community, in his evangelical charity, he reached out to everyone. Leaving behind his home, his family, the comfort of his familiar surroundings, he responded to the call to go forth, to speak of Christ wherever he was led. Saint Joseph knew how to offer the truth and the beauty of the Gospel in a multireligious context, with respect, dedication, perseverance, and humility. This is also the way for the followers of Jesus today. We are called to go forth with the same zeal, the same courage, of Saint Joseph Vaz, but also with his sensitivity, his reverence for others, his desire to share with them that word of grace [cf. Acts 20:32], which has the power to build them up. We are called to be missionary disciples."* We know Fr. Joseph Vaz was an Indian missionary, like ourselves, who journeyed to Sri

Lanka. This should be exactly the spirit of every priest who takes the challenges of traveling to a new country, away from his native and accustomed culture.

Ben: Brother, I confess once again that not like you, I in no way had a clear sense of such missionary spirit at the beginning of my life in the USA. My primary thought was to pursue my special postgraduate education in religious and social theater and communication in big cities like New York or Chicago. But God had his way. As he has been from the very beginning of my priestly formation, he did his best to transform me to be his worthy missionary servant in his kingdom. As intelligent as I could be, saluting to my own "naughty brain," to all its impulses and whims, I tried to dodge my Father's plan, and as one Oklahoman priest used to ridicule me (who really hurt me very much with his attitude and remarks), naming me a renegade. But my Prodigal Father never budgeted out of his master plan for me. He pursued me till this day and makes sure I am on the right track of serving Him only as a missionary. What should I say? "Father, if it is your will, let it be done to me according to your Word."

Dasan: Before we end our conversation, let us discuss a bit about the questionnaire you sent out and the answers received from your colleagues in the mission field. I went through all of them. on the answers to your question *"What are the reasons for your coming out of your native country and continuing priestly ministry in the USA?"* 90 percent of them, like me, say they were sent by their bishops or superiors; 10 percent of them, like you, respond they came for higher education and, with their superiors' consent, have stayed back to serve as missionaries in the USA; almost all of them agree they individually are attracted by America's appropriate environment of freedom and opportunity and its law-binding religious milieu to serve the church with soul satisfaction. A few also concede that they have chosen to stay and serve in America for they dare to test new waves of life, as you echoed the words of Pope Francis, *Avanti* ("Go beyond"). Some answer that they are here to give back what they have received from their American studies.

Ben: Let me add their answers to this question: "*Does your ministry in the USA make you feel grateful? Sorrowful? Joyful? Fulfilled? Regretful?* (I wanted them to rank their answers in the range of 1 to 10.) Very interestingly, practically everyone affirms they feel 100 percent fulfilled, grateful, and joyful. Not even a single priest notes he feels regretful. However, while everyone shares his sorrowful moments in their missionary pursuit, all, in one voice, state, as we have been sharing in previous chapters, that they are mature enough to take up these crosses, as Jesus did and expects from his disciples.

Dasan: Yes, Amalan, when we avow to conduct ourselves as Catholic missionaries in truth and Spirit, sufferings are part of our territory. In any situation, we are demanded of our Master to bring to people his Glad Tidings of truth, justice, love, peace, and purity. All of us, as missionaries, whether religious or diocesan, made promises and vows in front of God and the community of believers to be faithful to our special call to observe all evangelical values sincerely as our Master demands of his disciples. All for what? It's just to bring the Good News of God to the world vividly and straightforwardly. But unfortunately, throughout the church history, we notice so many of them could not bear the burden of such vowed life forever for many reasons, and therefore, they drifted away from their august call. A few among them accepted their weakness and confessed their sins privately and publicly. Some of them were punished by the church; some others were chastised by both their conscience and God himself, and a few others left the church and discontinued their evangelical work for which they had been chosen by God. There was a small group of men and women in that crowd who left the visible church and, with all honesty, released themselves from the ties of hard vows and discipline, which they couldn't bear, but stood on their ground to please the Lord and went on being his faithful missionaries. Very sadly, since this last category of missionaries, because of having no proper qualifications and other background in social life, couldn't cope with the world's demands and requirements to get their livelihood, their lives have become so pathetic and miserable. According to the church's norms, they were not offered any help either. Many died of starvation and chronic sicknesses.

Ben: Brother, at this juncture, we have to ponder also on the lives of the remaining missionaries ordained and elected in the Catholic Church. All those men and women you pointed out so far are only 10 percent of the Catholic missionaries. What about the other 90 percent majority? Church history proves except a very few, all the others violate all their vows as much as possible; many were known to the high authorities of the church. They were given pardon, sent to retreats and rehabilitation homes, and readmitted to the ministries. A few others were totally suspended from their missionary duty and kept in exclusion, or what may be called home prison, in their bishop's house. There are so many who boldly and with no conscience whatsoever do all kinds of perverted crimes, but they are so smart, so rich, and so influential that they can very easily be condoned by the authorities and the public as well.

Dasan: The modern media—though they may base all their undertakings on commercial, popular, and profit motivations—can be considered as God-given prophetic means to purify the church of today. Through their efforts, the church and its so-called "ordained and chosen" missionaries of Christ are made to be on their knees for their dishonesty, materialism, and untruthfulness to the Spirit. All these men and women consider the sacrament of reconciliation as their refuge to hide their secret affairs. In this blink milieu, it is very hard for a missionary like me to be indifferent and cold and self-centered. That is why, like you, I began my writing ministry about the true religion and spirituality that should be the base of every missionary. This book too, as I indicated in my invitation to join me as coauthor, is the outcome of such hunger and ache for enhancing the missionary life and ministry of every priest.

As a final personal note, I have to thank you so much for traveling with me both in good and bad time as well. You have always been my mentor in managing my missionary life. Whenever I was in dreary, desolate situation, feeling downhearted and depressed, you have shared with me some miraculous, power-filled words of Jesus, which I cherish and treasure in my computer as the golden gleanings; I read them aloud to myself in those critical moments and try to rise up and walk with the Master.

Dasan: Amalan, I too preserve those words of Jesus not only in my computer but also in my heart. I think the first set of words are portraying the privileges we as missionaries are endowed with: "*Turning to the disciples in private Jesus said, 'Blessed are the eyes that see what you see. For I say to you, many prophets and kings desired to see what you see, but did not see it, and to hear what you hear, but did not hear it*'" (Lk. 10:23–24). And Jesus also said, "*Whoever listens to you listens to me. Whoever rejects you rejects me. And whoever rejects me rejects the one who sent me*" (Lk. 10:16).

Ben: Let me add the second group of those positive words of Jesus. They are about the power he has armed me with: "*Whatever town you enter and they do not receive you, go out into the streets and say, 'The dust of your town that clings to our feet, even that we shake off against you.' Yet know this: the kingdom of God is at hand. I tell you, it will be more tolerable for Sodom on that day than for that town*" (Lk. 10:10–12).

"*And [behold] I am sending the promise of my Father upon you; but stay in the city until you are clothed with power from on high*" (Lk. 24:49).

"*But you will receive power when the Holy Spirit comes upon you, and you will be my witnesses in Jerusalem, throughout Judea and Samaria, and to the ends of the earth*" (Acts 1:8).

"*Whoever receives you receives me, and whoever receives me receives the one who sent me. Whoever receives a prophet because he is a prophet will receive a prophet's reward, and whoever receives a righteous man because he is righteous will receive a righteous man's reward. And whoever gives only a cup of cold water to one of these little ones to drink because he is a disciple—amen, I say to you, he will surely not lose his reward*" (Matt. 10:40–42).

I am so blessed to be a missionary in America, largely relying on those promises and convictions of our Lord Jesus and, surely, by the prayerful and wise and spiritual support bestowed by thousands of Christians I have been serving as well as by my fellow priests.